Production, Property & Power

MAKING SENSE OF THE ECONOMY

GORDON BORONOW

POL ECONCEPTS
New Canaan, CT
www.pol-econcepts.com

PRODUCTION, PROPERTY & POWER
GORDON BORONOW
ISBN: 978-1-7334634-9-2
Library of Congress Control Number: 2019912437

Editorial services by Barbara Munson, Munson Communications, munsoncommunications.com
PP&P Model: Graphic Design by Rick Mapes, rickmapesdesign.com
Cover and interior design by Monica Thomas for TLC Book Design, TLCBookDesign.com

IMAGE CREDITS: Pg 7 Declaration of Independence © Marcopolo9442 / DepositPhotos.com; **Pg 11** Leonard Nimoy Mr. Spock NBC Television [Public Domain]; **Pg 11** Captain Kirk NBC Television [Public Domain]; **Pg 13** Korea at Night NASA [Public Domain]; **Pg 17** 1883-CC Eagle Coin: Christian Gobrecht Image by Lost Dutchman Rare Coins [Public Domain]; **Pg 24** Hourglass © Kuzmafoto / DepositPhotos.com; **Pg 29** Balance Time and Money © Avdeev_80 / DepositPhotos.com; **Pg 34** Election Day © Leo Lintang / AdobeStock.com; **Pg 48** VIX Volatility Index-Historical Chart / www.macrotrends.net; **Pg 50** Space satellite © cookelma / DepositPhotos.com; **Pg 65** Friedrick Hayek © DickClarkMises / Wikimedia Commons / CC-BY-SA-3.0; **Pg 67** Subprime Mortgage Originations BoogaLouie [Public Domain]; **Pg 69** John Keynes IMF [Public Domain]; **Pg 70** Arthur Laffer Павел2010 [Public Domain]; **Pg 74** USA Social Security Cards © steveheap / DepositPhotos.com. **Pgs 14, 15, 16, 39, 46, 51, 55, 76** photos provided by Storyblocks Images, Storyblocks.com.

Printed in the United States of America

Contents

1

Foundational Concepts

In the Fall of 2008, as the financial crisis spread around the globe, I completed graduate school with a degree in economics. As the economy sank into recession, I realized that, despite my newly completed education, I did not really understand how the economy works. I determined to find out. As my understanding took shape, I developed this visual model of how the economy works, to make sense of the economy.

Is it even possible to understand the way the world works? Can we anticipate an economic crisis? Can we understand forces that produce such a wide range of outputs like Game of Thrones, Amazon, artificial intelligence or Obamacare, as just a few examples?

Yes, there is a limited sense in which we can understand the workings of the world we live in. We cannot comprehend it in all its complexity. But we see patterns in the interactions among people and institutions that play important roles in the economy. For example, people are naturally self-interested. We make economic decisions with our future well-being in mind, not simply our present welfare. We observe that people cooperate to produce a better life together. We know that there are evil forces at work in humans too, that must be properly contained to allow for human flourishing.

Our understanding begins with a mental framework or model of the way the world works. It is useful to have an expectation of how forces and events are likely to affect the economic choices people make. Will a proposed new policy lead to greater freedom and innovation; will it enhance the level of security in the economy? How might such a policy affect households, or businesses, or our future selves and offspring? A mental model of the way the whole economy works together can enhance our understanding and make us better equipped to handle the choices we will face in the future. That is the purpose of *Production, Property & Power: Making Sense of the Economy.*

WHAT IS THE ECONOMY?

The "economy" is a complex, dynamic community of decision-makers who jointly determine how to use the nation's resources—natural resources, human resources, and social resources—resulting in the production and consumption of goods and services of everyday life, plus the accumulation (or not) of wealth for the future.

An economy is complex because it involves billions of connections between millions of people in ways that are hard to anticipate. An economy is complex because decision-makers are human, with the full range of human motivations; from rigorous logic to a compelling "hunch," with traditions, duties and emotions tossed into the decision process for good measure. An economy is complex because the consequences of decisions made in one place ripple through the connected economy.

An economy is dynamic. Each decision leads to an outcome that becomes part of the accumulated learning of the whole. Learning will affect in some degree the next decision and the outcome of the next decision. Accumulated learning may lead to unintended outcomes. For example, a decision to cut tax rates may create an unintended outcome if the accumulated learning of taxpayers causes a rising anxiety about deficits and debt, which overwhelms the increased incentive to be more productive.

Dynamism is an important characteristic of an economy. A stagnant economy, in which every action has predictable outcomes, is an economy in which little learning is taking place. A stagnant economy is unlikely to produce innovations to improve everyday life. A highly controlled economy is going to be a stagnant economy, with little learning taking place. An economy in which people are free to experiment with innovations and are rewarded for successful outcomes is likely to expand collective learning and improve everyday life. A dramatic contrast between a controlled economy and a dynamic economy is the contrast between North and South Korea.

An economy is a community of households and institutions, workers and decision-makers. There is a structure to an economy that can be distinguished from one country to another. The structure is observed in the legal framework of the economy, in the political institutions, in the types of industry, and in the financial institutions and the living arrange-

ments of the people. Some economies are agricultural, some are industrial, and still others are knowledge-based. There is a discernable structure to the way institutions have organized themselves to produce and consume the stuff of everyday life.

For example, the United States is founded on principles of life, liberty and the pursuit of a life well-lived (i.e., happiness). Our economic structure is derived from these founding values. It is based on "markets," of which we will say more later. Here the emphasis is on the essential freedom of a market-oriented structure. Decision-makers and workers are free to produce whatever they want and sell it in the open market at whatever price the buyer and seller freely agree to. The essential freedom of the market-based structure of the economy is a direct reflection of liberty within the American political structure. To the extent there is a loss of political freedom, there is a loss of economic freedom, *and* vice versa.

Liberty is also reflected in the freedom to organize into producing companies, to choose how to spend our time, our money, and to choose where we want to work. Freedom increases dynamism and complexity in the economy. Therefore, more learning and innovation will take place in a free economy. The economic advances in China over the past thirty years are due in no small measure to the introduction of reforms that increased economic freedom in that economy.

The mental framework and visual model presented in this book will increase your understanding of the American market-based economy, acknowledging it is complex and dynamic. We must necessarily pare away complexity to better see the underlying structure of the economy: important connections between institutions and decision-makers of the economy. Let's call the pared-down mental framework of the economy the Production, Property & Power model, or the PP&P model for short. The reason for this name will become clear as you read on. The PP&P model has representative economic decision-makers: heads of households, entrepreneurs, bankers, and politicians. The pared-away institutional structure of the economy consists of the family (households), firms which produce consumer goods, firms which produce capital goods, banks, and government. (The distinction between firms which produce consumer goods versus firms which produce capital goods is not usually significant, but it does play a key role in understanding the process of innovation and growth.) Firms of all types are assumed to operate as efficiently as they can. The PP&P economy exists in a political environment that respects economic freedom and the rule of law.

The pared-down PP&P model of the economy will reveal much about how a complex and dynamic economy behaves. But do not be fooled. This simplified model can only capture a hint of the power and complexity of the real economy. The United States economy consists of 330 million people living and working in millions of families and companies spread over a continental-sized country. This simple model cannot possibly explain the miracle that is the US economy. But it can hopefully make a good start to understanding the basics.

HOW IS WEALTH CREATED?

The terms wealth and value are often used interchangeably. Wealth connotes accumulated value but when that distinction is not relevant, both terms are used interchangeably. The pared-down PP&P model includes three different ways in which wealth or value is created.

Exchange Value

Wealth is created when a good or service is traded for another good or service. Trade, by its voluntary nature, requires that each party to the trade be better off after making the exchange than it was before the exchange. Exchange surplus value, the sum of the increase in value experienced by both sides of the trade, involves a subtle concept that has been the subject of debate for centuries: what is the value of a good or service?

One view, which had a long history among economists prior to the twentieth century, is that the value of a good or service is based on the cost to produce the good or service. Some cost enters production directly as workers labor to produce the good and materials are used in the process. Some cost enters the production process indirectly through machines that were themselves produced.

The sum of all the costs incurred to produce the good (or service) is the value of that good. This view is known as the labor theory or the cost-of-production theory of value. Objects that cost more to produce must be more valuable. The producer wants to sell that good at a price higher than the cost of production. Intuitively, this view makes sense. But this cannot be the whole story. Simply adding cost to the production of a good does not make it more valuable.

In the 1870s, an alternative theory of value was developed. The new theory claimed that value is subjective. Value, like beauty, is in the eye and mind of the beholder. Each person has their own opinion as to the value of a specific good or service. For example, a painting may be highly prized by one person and hold no attraction to another. A person shopping for new clothes might decide that a new line of fashion is worth the higher price, while another shopper is content with last year's style on the clearance rack. Value is the subjective evaluation of the potential buyer.

The seller's production cost measure of value and the buyer's subjective opinion of value are reconciled in the free market. The seller searches the market to find a buyer whose appraisal of value is greater than the seller's cost of production. If the seller finds such a buyer, an exchange is possible that is profitable to both parties. The price they ultimately agree upon will be lower than what the buyer thinks the good is worth and higher than the seller's cost of production. Both buyer and seller win. It is reasonable to say that the selling price is the value of the good, even though the price is neither the cost of production nor the subjective assessment of the buyer. It is the value determined by free people engaging in free exchange.

Exchange is an action that increases the well-being of both parties, i.e., that creates wealth. Each party willingly parts with something in exchange for something of greater value (to themselves). Wealth creation via exchange is ubiquitous. Workers voluntarily exchange their time, talents, and energy for a freely agreed wage. The wage is worth more to the worker than alternative uses of time. The worker's production is worth more to the employer than the wage. They are both better off after the exchange. (They are not necessarily equally better off. One party may get a better deal.) A shopper at Macy's creates wealth when he buys a new shirt for $30. We cannot read the mind of the buyer, so we don't know exactly what the value of the shirt is to him, but we do know that in his opinion the shirt is worth more than $30. Macy's is better off, too. Macy's set the price.

Innovation and Learning

Another way value is created is through innovation and learning. Innovation is the discovery and implementation of new ideas: ideas for new products, new uses for old products, better ways to produce old products using a better mix of resources or processes. Learning is the increase in productivity that occurs as a person becomes more skillful at their job through training, practice, and experience. Either through learning or through innovation, a person can become more productive; that is, he or she can produce the same output with fewer inputs of time or resources. More value is created than before. Thus, innovation and learning are a second path to value creation.

Creating value through innovation and learning is not a simple matter. New ideas do not just spring from the mind of the innovator to the factory production floor. Learning does not happen overnight. Both require an investment of time and resources to bring new ideas or new learning into existence. There is no guarantee that the investment will be fruitful. Many ideas do not work out and the investment is lost. Much learning is wasted effort. The path of innovation and investment is a risky path. But "the market" rewards the courageous entrepreneur if the innovation is successful. Likewise, "the market" rewards learning through a willingness to pay higher wages for higher productivity.

Ethical Conduct

A third way to create wealth and preserve wealth is through society-wide adherence to a rule of law under a high standard of ethical conduct. Imagine a society without a rule of law or without widespread ethical conduct. A dog-eat-dog existence would be the outcome, with a high cost to simply preserve the safety of life and property. In such a society, wealth would be hard to create or preserve.

An ethical society requires a healthy culture in which ethical values are formed. Ethical values are developed in families, churches, schools, and playgrounds. In the United States, "We the people" authorize government to produce justice and protect liberty. If justice and security are assured and if people live according to common ethical standards, then trust grows and the community flourishes. Rule of law is the even-handed application of government power to punish those who break the rules. Law supports an ethical society; it is a very poor substitute for ethical conduct. Rule of law is much better when it is complementary to high ethical standards, producing a healthy social environment in which free people are able to innovate and flourish.

Usually, economists take a healthy social environment as given. That may be mostly true in the United States, a legacy from earlier generations. However, a healthy social environment does not just magically appear. It is produced over generations by social institutions; especially well-functioning families, churches, schools, and government. Without a healthy social environment, it is unlikely that a well-functioning economy can be sustained.

Value creation occurs in more ways than the three activities discussed above: exchange, innovation, and ethical conduct protected by the rule of law. However, these three ways to create wealth are highly relevant to the pared-down PP&P model economy. Each of these three paths to value creation corresponds to one of the three cycles of economic activity (Production, Property & Power) in the PP&P model. But there are still a few more foundational concepts to discuss before we get to the model.

HOW DO PEOPLE MAKE DECISIONS?

A good method for thinking about complex systems is to start one's analysis with simple assumptions. So economists often assume that people make decisions solely based on which outcome best advances their own self-interest. Based on this (highly) simplifying assumption, economists then analyze how such a person would choose to act. This hypothetical representation of a self-interested decision-making person is sometimes cheekily referred to as *homo economicus*, a shorthand way to state that the simplifying assumption above is in effect.

If such a person ever existed, they might be like Mr. Spock of *Star Trek* fame. No emotion, only perfect logic and reason would guide them to their decisions. *Homo economicus* is not a warm and caring person whose company you would enjoy. Fortunately, *homo economicus* does not exist; he is only a simplifying device. Real people are not only interested in themselves, they respect their duty to others and to society. Real people have emotions and passions. Real people do not have perfect reasoning abilities and often have limited information on which to

make decisions. In short, we are humans like Captain Kirk, not Vulcans like Mr. Spock.

While economists realize that *homo economicus* does not exist, they do insist that people act rationally. That is, people have a reason for the decisions they make and actions they take. The reason may be delusional, or hard to figure out, but somewhere in the mind of each person there is a reason for the choices they make. Therefore, it is convenient and useful (and not infrequently close to truth) to assume that people act like *homo economicus*. It makes economic analysis much easier.

In the Production, Property & Power model there are four decision-making characters who represent the decision-makers in the economy. While they have some resemblance to *homo economicus*, each of the four characters has human emotions. Therefore, they make decisions based on reason *and* emotion, in a pared-down way, as we shall see.

Usually, economists simply assume that decision-makers are adults with sound reasoning abilities and good judgment, are well-socialized, and have good ethical values. Some economists have analyzed how predicted economic outcomes might change if decision-makers are assumed to be affected by human foibles, such as impatience, or fearfulness, or inconsistency. But there has been surprisingly little attention among economists about how society produces mature and ethical decision-making adults.

One economist who did tackle this question is Jennifer Roback Morse in her book *Love and Economics: It Takes a Family to Raise a Village*. She makes a compelling argument for the importance of a loving family, a mother and a father, together with church or synagogue, in transforming a baby into a well-socialized adult with good judgment and ethical values. This is an example of critically important value creation, which lies outside the scope of the Production, Property & Power model. Like most economists, the PP&P model also takes well-adjusted decision-makers as given. But let us acknowledge the magnitude of that assumption.

WHAT ROLE DO "MARKETS" PLAY IN THE ECONOMY?

Markets are characteristic of a free economy. There are stock markets, labor markets, supermarkets, fish markets, oil markets, housing markets, car markets, and on and on and on. The connection between free economies and markets is so tight that a free economy is usually called a "free-market economy."

Consider an alternative to a free economy: a "command economy," which is centrally controlled. In a command economy, decisions about what to produce, who works on production, who consumes the production, what investments to make, and almost every other important decision is made by a centralized authority. Workers are assigned to jobs, production goals are set, raw materials are allocated, and consumption choices regarding food, clothing, housing, and even entertainment are issued from a central planning "czar." The whole economy is organized and directed from a powerful central command.

In contrast, there is no central planning authority in a free economy. Economic activity is directed according to decentralized learning that takes place in a multitude of free markets. This guide is not a critique of unfree economies. But it is easily observed that where economies are free, the people tend to flourish, and where economies are not free, the people tend to live lives of misery—South Korea vs. North Korea being Exhibit A.

Markets are the means in a free economy by which economic activity is guided to the best use of resources to satisfy the diverse wants of the people. This is a remarkable achievement. After all, markets are nothing more than physical or virtual places where buyers and sellers gather to choose whether to do business or not. How can something so simple guide the whole economy to the best use of resources? It is very easy to overlook the fundamentally important role that markets play in an economy. Therefore, before we look at how the PP&P model works, let's look more closely at how markets work in three examples of market-guided activities.

Market for Goods

The first example is a market for clothes. There are many clothing markets, including department stores, Main St. boutiques, catalogues, consignment shops, Amazon, etc. Any place, either physical or virtual, where buyers of clothing can do business with sellers of clothing is part of the "clothing market." Sellers display their goods, on racks or in pictures and words, along with a price they are asking for the clothes. Buyers browse through the racks, the catalog or the website. Buyers take into consideration styles, seasonality, colors,

sizes, durability, and many other factors that affect their opinion of value of the goods on display. They decide whether the good being offered for sale is the best use of their clothing budget. They choose to buy it or not.

If a sale is made, the seller learns they made successful decisions regarding the production and pricing of that piece of clothing. They can continue to produce that article of clothes, and perhaps even adjust the price a little higher next time. If the buyer chooses not to buy the clothing, the seller learns something too. The seller learns he or she needs to adjust something in the production of the clothing, or seek out a different type of buyer, or perhaps even reduce the asking price of the clothing. The seller may learn that their product cannot be sold for a high enough price to be profitable. The adjustment is to stop producing that garment.

The clothing market, like all markets, is a place of discovery and learning. The seller learns what the buyer is looking for and is willing to pay. Supply is adjusted to meet demand. The voluntary choices of buyer and seller, as revealed in the market, guide society to produce the clothes people are willing to buy.

Market for Workers

A different example of how markets work their magic is seen in labor markets. Labor markets run the gamut from markets to hire day-laborers to job-search firms for rocket scientists. Let's consider the market for nurses. The buyers (aka employers) of nursing services are hospitals, schools, doctor offices, long-term care facilities, home care networks, summer camps, and so on. In many cases employers are looking for special skills or training in such areas as emergency care, or pediatrics, or cardio-pulmonary care, etc. In labor markets it is the buyer, i.e., the employer, who usually offers a specified price, referred to as wage or salary. The seller of nursing services is the prospective nurse-employee. The seller, i.e., the prospective employee, evaluates the attractiveness of the opportunities offered by employers: such as the job location, wage offer, fringe benefits, training and advancement prospects, time flexibility, and whatever else they consider important. Then the seller for example, (the nurse) chooses to apply for a job with one of the employers. Or not. Next, the employer evaluates the applicants for their job offerings. The buyer selects the seller-applicant it deems the best fit with the job.

Once again, the labor market, like all markets, is a place of discovery and learning. The employer learns whether the specific offer of location, flexibility, wages and fringe benefits, prospects for advancement, and so on, is good enough to attract qualified candidates. If not, the buyer/employer learns that something needs to be adjusted to make the offer more attractive. Perhaps the wage offered is not high enough, perhaps the work hours need to be more flexible (or more predictable). Something needs to be adjusted to make the offer more acceptable to prospective nurses. At the second stage of the hiring process, the seller/nurse learns whether his/her set of skills is strong enough to get the job. If so, then other nurses will learn what is required to win similar jobs. If not, the seller/ nurse will learn that his collection of skills, training, and experience is not adequate and needs to be adjusted. Perhaps more training, different creden-

tials, or more experience at a less desirable job is needed to win the hiring competition. The seller/ nurse makes the necessary adjustments and applies for another job opportunity with another buyer/ employer.

Through the market process of discovery and learning, employ-ers of nursing services adjust their offerings to attract the best candidates, and nurses adjust their array of skills and experience to get the best job. The market guides buyers and sellers to the best outcomes.

Financial Markets

Consider one more example of how decentralized free markets guide economic activity: the market for investment funds. These markets are especially complex, with many diverse offerings of investment products and services. Consider the example of a company that seeks to raise funds for an expansion in the business. The company plans to spend the money over a two-year period to complete the expansion project, after which it expects to earn additional profits over the subsequent ten years. The company believes the project will earn a significant overall profit.

In financial markets, the company is the buyer/borrower of investment funds, and a lender is the seller of investment funds. There are many other buyers/borrowers in the market also seeking to borrow money for investment. There are many different types of sellers/lenders of investment funds. Some of the lenders are offering money for a short period of time, some for a few years, and some are willing to lend money for a long period of time. Some lenders will only lend money to borrowers who have very strong businesses and are nearly certain to repay the loan. Other sellers are willing to lend money to companies that are not as well established. In this market, the company/borrower considers the terms of loans offered by the sellers/lenders. The company decides which lender's offer is going to fit their need for funds and their willingness to pay the interest rate being asked. They apply for a loan from that lender. Next the seller/lender evaluates the credit-worthiness of the borrower, and the likelihood of a successful project, relative to the applications for other projects from other potential borrowers. The lender approves the loan application (or not) and the buyer gets the loan (or not).

A discovery process takes place in the market. Potential borrowers choose the most attractive loan offers. Lenders learn what adjustments they need to make if they want to attract more borrowers. In the second phase of the market process, lenders choose the most attractive applications from among potential borrowers. Borrowers learn whether they need to adjust their projects to be more profitable, or consider shorter payback periods. If they cannot get the funds they seek, they may have to abandon their project entirely. The market guides the economy so that investment funds are made available to the best projects, with the most potential for success.

These examples illustrate discovery and learning that takes place in free markets. Feedback from countless market interactions guides buyers and sellers to adjustments that increase their chances of successful market outcomes. There is no central planning authority, only buyers and sellers voluntarily doing business together, guiding the economy to the best outcomes. Markets are truly amazing.

There are critics who disagree and claim that markets do not guide society to the best outcomes. They point to "market failures," such as pollution, where market-based competition and interaction of buyers and sellers does not produce an acceptable outcome. They argue that centralized control is needed to prevent or correct "market failure." A free society needs to debate these questions. On a case-by-case basis, society needs to choose the best way to prevent or minimize potential for market failure, including the option for central control. However, society needs to be cautious that the "fix" does not lead to even more harmful "government failure." (Government failure occurs when a law or regulation leads to corruption or to other consequences that are harmful to society. For example, rent control laws easily result in corruption and worsening shortages of affordable, decent housing.) The economy of the United States is a mix of market-guided activity and government-directed activity.

WHAT ABOUT MONEY?

"Sound Money" Assumption

Obviously, money is a key element to any economy. In fact, money is one of the most challenging subjects for students in economics. It is well beyond the scope of this guide. In the Production, Property & Power model, money is simply assumed to be "sound money," that is, money is assumed to maintain its purchasing power over time. Thus, we will not consider the effects of inflation or the complications of floating exchange rates that are used to trade currencies with other countries. We will simply ignore these significant complications, and assume money is sound money.

To put that assumption into some context, sound money is like gold coins during the period of a gold standard. A gold standard has its own problems, but it acted to preserve purchasing power quite well. Alternatively, sound money is like assuming the

Federal Reserve Bank controls the rate of inflation to be 0%, year after year. (The Federal Reserve Bank, known as the Fed, is the institution authorized by Congress to manage the value of money in the United States.)

In fact, money does not maintain its purchasing power from year to year. The Fed's stated objective is to control the value of money so that inflation is 2% per year. If the Fed is successful, money will lose 2% of its value every year. Inflation distorts the ability of decision-makers to make long-term decisions. Inflation in an economy is like driving a car through fog. If the fog is not too thick, you only need to slow down. Long-term decisions are still possible, but they involve more risk. But if you are in a deep fog (i.e., out-of-control inflation), driving at all becomes very dangerous; long-term money decisions are reckless.

The Fed, especially since the end of the gold-based money system in 1971, manages money with an eye to the health of the overall economy. This aspect of monetary policy is beyond the scope of the Production, Property & Power model. The pared-down PP&P model assumes the Fed is "neutral"; neither trying to boost the economy with "easy" money conditions, nor trying to slow down the economy with "tight" money conditions. In our model the Fed is assumed to do one thing only: keep inflation at zero. Nothing more.

Money as Money

While on the subject, it is worth a brief look at the importance of money as money, not as a policy tool to manage the economy. Money as money plays three important roles in the economy. First, money makes trade and exchange possible. Remember how exchange value is created by every trade. Without money, it would be difficult to create value through trade/exchange. Barter, the default method of trade without money, is simply not an effective basis for widespread trade, especially for complex trades that occur between multiple parties. With the use of money, trade can easily extend beyond the confines of barter between two parties. Commerce among many parties with a wide variety of goods to exchange is made possible.

Money is used to measure the relative value of apples compared to oranges. We can easily understand relative values when money prices are available. It takes a year of work to pay for a car or for tuition at college. If you eat peanut butter sandwiches for two months, you can afford a week's vacation at the beach. These comparisons are made possible by using money to measure relative value.

Finally, money easily transports purchasing power through space (from New York to Los Angeles) and time (from now to next week or next year or to retirement). This feature of money is called a "store of value," meaning that money stores purchasing power until it is called upon to use it. Money is like a bucket, carrying purchasing power to where it is wanted. If the bucket has holes in it, it cannot do its job very well. So it is with money. Unless money is sound money, it cannot do its job very well as a store of value. Our model of the economy assumes there is no inflation; i.e., there are no holes in the bucket.

The importance of money as a store of value is often under-appreciated. If money is a leaky bucket, that is, if inflation is rampant, or if money wealth is heavily taxed, or if money is likely to be stolen, then people will find other forms of property to be a store of value. People will buy gold, jewelry, rare artwork, exotic cars and so on as a place to store purchasing power outside the reach of inflation or the tax collector or the thief. These alternative stores of value are often inert; wealth is imprisoned in exotic stores of value, adding nothing to the productive capacity of the economy. But when money is a sound and reliable store of value, it can be put to work as a financial asset for investment in productive enterprises, adding to the wealth-creating power of the economy.

WRAP-UP

We have considered foundational elements of the economy that are operating in the background of the PP&P model. The model we are about to explore is a model of a free market economy, in a society governed by the rule of law with widespread ethical conduct. Value creation occurs through market-based free exchanges that guide the production and consumption of a wide variety of goods and services. Value creation (and destruction) also occurs through investment in learning and innovation, a risky process in which new skills and ideas are developed at the cost of time and resources. If successful, innovation and learning create value. If not successful, the time and resources used for innovation and learning are wasted. Finally, wealth is preserved by the actions of government to secure justice, life and property with rule of law. Good government enhances the well-being of society. Too much government intervention in the economy however, can be harmful to society due to increased potential for government failure, i.e., corruption, incompetence or unexpected harmful outcomes.

The Production, Property & Power model is populated by human decision-makers, who have human strengths and foibles. We assume they have good judgment, not perfect reasoning abilities. Voluntary economic transactions take place in markets government directed activities take place in the political sphere. Money is assumed to be sound and not manipulated to manage the economy, which manages itself.

2

The Economy Is About People

E conomics is a behavioral science. It is a study of the way people use resources. Even when economics turns into statistical analysis or is formulated into mathematical relationships, at its core economics is still about people. And that makes economics interesting.

We cannot fully understand the economy, because people are too complex and dynamic for us to fully understand. But we can reflect on our own experiences to predict how people in the world around us are likely to behave. We construct a story of what is likely to happen in the economy. Then we compare that story to what we observe happening and make corrections to the story. This is how economists have always worked, even as economics has evolved, for better or worse, into the mathematical discipline it largely is today.

This is a story then of how the economy works. People make choices for themselves and for institutions they control, based on a rational process of decision-making. Even rational people are not always predictable because their reasons are often hidden from view. The story uses terms like *expectations* and likelihood to acknowledge the essential uncertainty of economics. The story explains how decisions made in one part of the economy affect other sectors of the economy. If we understand these connections, we are better able to evaluate how changes in public policy might affect the future.

Here we use a pared-down illustrated model of the economy to tell our story, the Production, Property & Power Model. There are four different types of decision-making people in our story: people in households living life, business entrepreneurs with innovative ideas, bankers who finance innovation, and politicians who use the power of government to "do good." These representative characters have goals, feelings, challenges. The model predicts how they might behave, and what is likely to happen in the economy if they behave according to our story.

Let's get to know the characters better.

HEADS OF HOUSEHOLDS

Meet Jack, the head of household for the Smith family. Jack and Lori have two kids, and a mortgage. He is planning to retire from his account management job in about 20 years, and he is counting on Social Security to provide half his retirement income. Jack is worried; he read that Social Security is running out of money. Jack is trying to figure out how to balance what the family wants to buy today with potential needs he and Lori will face in retirement. (Jack and Lori have a child in college, and the other one is planning to get married next year.)

Role/Decisions

The head of household is assumed to be the decision-maker for the household. Economists often select the head of household as the decision-maker in their stories, rather than the individual members of the household. It is reasonable to focus on the head of household, since major elements of economic life such as housing, food, and transportation are usually consumed as a household. It is also reasonable to assume that the decision-maker for the household incorporates the interests of the whole household into the choices he/she makes on behalf of the household. Much of the available statistical data, therefore, is collected and reported at the household level, not at the level of individuals.

There is a wide diversity of households in the economy, highlighting a weakness of the pared-down model. Traditional families like the Smiths make up less than 25% of households in America. Nonetheless, in the PP&P model, Jack represents heads of all the diverse households. Simplicity demands such parsimony.

Each household spends money on consumer goods and services and saves money in anticipation of the needs of the future household. A key decision facing the head of the household is how much to save for the future, and how much can be used for purchases now. The save-or-spend decision takes account of all resources at the disposal of the household; past (savings), present (income), and future (borrowing).

Decision-maker Jack makes up a budget for purchases of goods and services. What is not spent is saved, adding to the "nest egg" wealth that has accumulated over the prior years. The accumulated wealth will be available to a future household decision-maker (probably Jack again) next year. Wealth consists of property; physical property such as land, house or jewelry, but also financial property such as stocks, bonds, savings accounts, and so on. Households are the ultimate owners of all non-government assets (at least in the model). Firms may own assets, but households own the firms.

Jack's household (together with all the other households) supply workers for the economy, both to firms and to the government. Another key decision of the household is how to spend their available time. Some time is used to work and earn income, while some time is used for leisure activities. The decision to work or not to work is motivated by the desire to earn an income balanced by a desire to enjoy leisure. People work for many important reasons other than simply to earn money. Work gives dignity, an outlet for creativity, and many other reasons. But for the sake of simplicity, we ignore all other reasons to work than to earn an income. In Jack's situation, he chooses to work several hours of overtime each week to help pay for college and prepare for the upcoming wedding.

Finally, households pay taxes to the government. Jack has no choice in the matter. The household does not choose how much to pay in taxes. That choice is made by government. The only thing that Jack can choose is to work longer to pay for the tax, or to work less to spend his time on untaxed activities. In the PP&P story, the household has no role in the choice of government. Government is just a given fact of life.

In the PP&P model, households pay taxes but firms do not pay taxes. There is a saying among economists that "firms do not pay taxes, they merely collect them." The point is that the burden of taxes on a firm is passed along to people; either customers (higher prices), employees (lower take-home pay) or owners (lower profits). The tax burden falls differently among customers, workers, and owners depending on the relative market power of the customer, employee and owner in any given firm. Nonetheless, the tax burden is borne by a person who lives in a household. Therefore, in the PP&P model, only households pay taxes.

Time

The decision-maker of the household does not make choices for today only, based on some mental calculus of present pleasures. Rather, Jack makes each decision based on the likely impact on the household in the near and distant future, as well as today. Household choices have a future dimension; should I  buy green bananas, how much to save for retirement, or whether to buy or rent a house. The decision-maker must analyze incredibly complex future options and arrive at the best choice for saving or spending at this moment in time.

Perhaps more than any other aspect of the economy, the time dimension is the most difficult aspect for economists to analyze. Certainly, economists have long recognized the time dimension in economics. Psychologists have shown that different people evaluate time differently. While we cannot know how, we can say for sure that the decision-maker evaluates the future when making present day decisions.

When circumstances change, the household decision-maker (Jack) can abruptly change his outlook from confident about the future to anxious about the future. One day Jack may decide to buy a new car. The next day Jack hears of layoffs in the purchasing department and he decides not to spend any more money than is necessary. He cancels the new car order and looks at used cars. While economy-wide household spending is large and quite stable, there can be relatively large swings in the much smaller amount of savings by the households as the heads of households adjust to a changing outlook.

Economists often use a theoretical technique called "the steady-state," or "equilibrium," to analyze the economy. When an economy is in equilibrium, or steady-state, decision-makers across the economy on average make the same choices period after period. On average they spend the same portion of resources and save the same portion each year. There is nothing happening that would cause decision-makers to deviate from the choices made last period. The whole system calms down, like the surface of a pond long after a pebble has fallen into it. In steady-state, "time" is irrelevant since nothing changes. Steady-state analysis hides the importance of time to the economy. In fact, time is highly relevant; change happens and it takes time to adjust to change.

Even if the political world and the economy were incredibly stable (which they are not), the forces of nature and mortality would still make the future unknowable. And of course, the world is not stable. Heads of household like Jack must assess information about the future and adjust their today choices accordingly, to do their best for the current and future household.

The Best Choice

What does it mean to say that a choice is the "best" choice? How does Jack decide what is best? Consider a car, for example. Is the best car the one with the lowest price? The car most likely to reach 200,000 miles? The car with the highest safety rating? The one with the least impact on the environment? Is it the car with the highest "cool factor"? Each household has its own preferences (i.e., likes, values, and emotions that affect the choice). One household may emphasize frugality, another household is safety-minded, and yet another household is passionate about environmental considerations. There is no single "best." *Best* is specific to each household, based on what is most important to it.

Economists use a concept called "utility" to measure what is "best." Loosely speaking, utility is a measure of the degree of satisfaction, happiness, or usefulness a good or service provides to the consumer. Utility reduces multiple sources of satisfaction and preferences into a single conceptual measure. For example, the family-oriented car buyer will probably derive more utility from safety features than it would from the fact that the car can go from 0 to 60 miles per hour in 4.3 seconds. For the environmentally minded, a low carbon footprint generates higher utility than a low price. Jack will choose the car that generates the most utility compared to the utility generated through other possible choices.

The utility mechanism has challenges. Utility cannot be measured in absolute units. Utility can only be measured in comparison to other choices; that car generates more utility than this car. Utility has many sources. A person will derive utility from the pleasure of consumption, from the pleasure of sharing, from doing one's work well, from observing beauty, from creating something new, from achieving a difficult objective, etc. Economic models usually assume that the pleasures of consumption (present and future) generate much greater utility than other sources of utility. This assumption is made only because it makes the models much easier to analyze. But it implies that humans care much more about their own material consumption (and that of their household) than other motivations in life, such as the common good, friendship, beauty, or whatever. While not very flattering, on average, the assumption works relatively well for many purposes.

But assuming that utility comes from materialistic consumption alone is inadequate to understand the way the economy works. It gives us only the most superficial understanding of the economy. To make the story more realistic, we must consider disutility (the opposite of utility) generated by fear and insecurity. Fear and insecurity are powerful motivators that can disrupt decisions that might have been made if fear or insecurity were not present. Households derive utility from choices that reduce fear and insecurity, and disutility comes from choices that increase fear and insecurity. Sometimes a choice may generate both utility from consumption and disutility from insecurity. For example, an expensive vacation may generate both utility from the enjoyment of the vacation, and disutility from anxiety about affordability.

Thus, even in this pared-down story of the economy, we have two motivating forces affecting the mind of the decision-maker: satisfaction from the enjoyment of consumption and reduction of fear and insecurity. It is a complex interaction as to which force prevails as Jack makes his decision. When Jack chooses to spend on consumption today, the utility from consumption must be greater than the utility from more savings, which would reduce anxiety about the future. But if Jack's feelings of fear and uncertainty are prominent, then he will choose to add to savings (and thereby reduce fear and insecurity) instead of spending on consumption. Jack will choose to "tighten his belt."

The same type of utility analysis can be applied to Jack's decisions about how many hours he will choose to work and how many hours he will choose to do something else. The longer he works, the greater his income. More income can generate utility by reducing the anxiety that Jack is feeling about his situation. But Jack also gets utility from using his time to enjoy life; time with the family, golf with friends, even from cutting the grass. Jack balances the utility from using time to earn more income to reduce anxiety against the utility he could enjoy from spending his time living life. (In reality, Jack's ability to adjust work hours may be limited, but within limits, Jack does have room to make these tradeoffs.)

A desire to reduce fear and insecurity is why people welcome more government into the economy. This is true despite the heavy price of government in taxes and potential loss of freedom. It is a stretch to claim that households choose to "consume" more government services over say, a better car. Households have very little choice in how much government they get to "consume." It is more realistic to recognize that households seek to reduce fear and increase security, so they empower government by their taxes. The more fear and anxiety they feel, the more willing people are to give government power. Which is why governments extend their power in a crisis. Which is also why politicians always tell us how bad things are and how much better they can make the situation, if only…

Unlike the stable satisfaction of consumption, the forces of fear and insecurity are quite volatile. Fear can pop up suddenly in response to events, or even rumors of events. We observe sudden changes in household choices. There must be a force acting on decision-makers besides the utility of consumption to account for the sudden change. That other force is disutility from fear and insecurity triggered by unexpected events.

Summary of the Household Decision-maker

The choices made by the head of household decision-maker drive the economy. The head of household chooses what to consume and what to save. He/she also chooses how much to work and how much leisure time to enjoy. Each household is unique, having diverse labor skills, income, wealth, and preferences. But there are commonalities on which we build a model of the economy. First, the household does not exist only in the present; the present head of household anticipates the needs and desires of an expected future household. Second, households make decisions that are "best" for them. The "best" choice balances utility from consumption (now and future) and utility from a reduction of fear and insecurity (now and future).

Adam Smith, the father of modern economics, said in *The Theory of Moral Sentiments,* "Every man is, no doubt, by nature, first and principally recommended to his own care; and as he is fitter to take care of himself than of any other person, it is fit and right that it should be so." We tip our hat to the wise household decision-maker.

ENTREPRENEURS

The opportunity for change, innovation, and growth is created by courageous decisions of entrepreneurs to undertake the risk involved in making something new.

Role/Decisions

The Production, Property & Power Model (PP&P) makes a distinction between the productive role of the firm, and the change-making role of the entrepreneur. As efficiently as possible, the firm produces goods and services: which goods and services to produce, how much to produce, and what processes to use in production.

The firm also decides what to do with earnings, if any, after it has paid all its costs, including the cost of labor, materials, and interest on debt. Should the firm pay the residual earnings to the owners in the form of a dividend, or should it retain the earnings to reinvest in business innovation? Enter the entrepreneur.

This is Tom, the head of engineering at Acme Manufacturing Co. Like most entrepreneurs in the modern economy, Tom works for a company, Acme, to make them a more successful company. Sure, he knows of entrepreneurs that start their own firms, but Tom is happy right where he is. He's had a few great ideas over the years, and he has been rewarded with bonuses and promotions (unlike his friend Joe, who "retired" last year when his latest invention bombed in the market). Now he is working on an idea that would replace Acme's most popular product with brand new technology. The first problem to overcome is that it will take a lot of money to test the technology and build a new production line. After Joe's fiasco, Acme does not have enough earnings after dividends are paid, to finance the development of his ground-breaking idea.

When the entrepreneur needs resources for an innovation or expansion, he or she faces the difficult task of raising money. Since Acme does not have enough retained earnings to fully fund the project, Tom will have to get additional funds elsewhere.

Driven to Profitable Innovation

Entrepreneurs like Tom are motivated to turn ideas into profitable outcomes; it is the company's path to survival. There will be profits only when the consumer is willing to buy the newly developed product (or service or process) at a price high enough to cover the cost of production plus a return on capital needed for development. Otherwise there will be losses. This is the self-correcting mechanism of capitalism. Entrepreneurs frequently make mistakes—produce an unwanted product or use a too-costly production process. That is what happened with Joe. Mistakes are corrected quickly in a free market system;

otherwise the firm goes out of business. Tom spends his working life searching for new ways to make products that are valuable to consumers, or to produce them at lower cost, or to invent new products entirely. He is motivated not only by rewards from profits, but also out of fear that a competitor will discover something new and better before he does. That would be bad for Tom, and bad for Acme. Something new and better would be good for consumers, however.

It is undoubtedly true that some entrepreneurs create new products and innovations for the joy of creativity. But it is convenient and reasonable to assume that entrepreneurs are motivated mostly by the lure of future profits or the fear that competitors will put them out of business.

In the course of development, entrepreneurs might have to build new factories, buy new equipment, use new materials and methods, and so on. Business investment is risky; costly mistakes are possible. Done well, the entrepreneur gives birth to new products, increased productivity, wealth, and higher living standards in the economy overall. Done poorly, the entrepreneur wastes scarce resources, reducing wealth. The free market process rewards good outcomes with profits and bad outcomes with losses. This market-tested discipline makes it more likely that resources are used effectively.

Time

Time is a major consideration for the entrepreneur just as it is for the household decision-maker. The entrepreneur is forward-looking, anticipating profits from innovation. Innovation is inherently risky, since the future is unknown. The entrepreneur (and potential investors) must consider changes that might occur during the time it takes to develop his new idea. Someone else might  develop a better idea; there might be new regulations, an uncertain outlook for necessary government permits, new tax rules, political upheaval, etc. The potential for adverse change increases with time. Projects that can be developed quickly (such as the introduction of a pumpkin spice latte) are more easily financed at a relatively low cost of funds. Projects that require a long time to complete (such as a driverless delivery truck) are difficult to finance, with a relatively high cost of funds.

Time-related risk also means that sudden shocks to the economy have a volatile effect on the entrepreneur, just as they do on the household. The plans of the entrepreneur are disrupted. Projects might be cancelled or postponed. In some cases, projects that were rejected because they were unprofitable become feasible due to a change in conditions. (For example, an unexpected government subsidy may suddenly make a solar energy project feasible.) Forward-looking entrepreneurs change their outlook quickly as they respond to shocks in the economy, or even to rumors.

Summary of the Entrepreneur

Entrepreneurs are forward-looking innovators who anticipate demand for new products or services, or who visualize new and better processes. Entrepreneurs must raise funds to develop their ideas; either from the retained earnings of an existing firm or by attracting financial backers. This requires potential for future profits. When an uncertain future becomes more uncertain due to economic shocks, or lengthy completion time, or politically driven policy change, it becomes even more difficult to evaluate future profits and therefore more difficult to raise funds for new business investments. When the future outlook appears more stable and predictable, it becomes easier to evaluate future profits and easier to find sources of funds for business investment. Nonetheless, business investment is inherently risky, involving the fickle fate of time.

THE BANKER

Once Tom, the entrepreneur, comes up with a blockbuster idea, his next challenge is to obtain the funds required to develop the idea into reality. In the historical past, entrepreneurs would seek government support or funds from wealthy patrons. The modern free economy offers another alternative: the financial industry. The financial industry includes many institutions, such as mutual funds, brokerages, and pension funds, but in the pared-down PP&P model the entire financial industry will be represented by a bank.

A bank accepts checking and savings account deposits from households and lends the aggregated funds to entrepreneurs. (A bank also makes consumer loans to households, but our focus here is on business investments.) Interest earned on the business loans pays the cost of interest paid to the depositors plus the other expenses and profits of the bank.

Like all firms, banks need to be profitable to survive. Profits depend on the ability of banks to attract deposits from households and carefully lend those funds to entrepreneurs. If banks select successful projects to finance with business loans, and avoid making loans to projects that fail, then the bank can be profitable. Therefore, banks need people with good judgment and deep understanding of business to carefully select which projects are worthy of financing.

Janet, the banker in the Production, Property & Power model is such a person. The bank relies on Janet to analyze each loan request and approve the projects she believes are the most likely to be fully repaid with interest. (Note: The approved loans are not necessarily the "best" ideas but they are projects Janet is convinced will not default.) The bank also counts on Janet to reject loan applications for projects that are too risky; that is, the projects that are least likely to be successful.

Janet uses logical methods and proven algorithms to identify the projects most likely to be profitable. But Janet is human, not simply a risk-calculating algorithm. Janet uses business savvy to improve the outcomes of the lending process. Therefore, as Keynes famously pointed out, Janet is subject to "animal spirits." That is, she becomes overly cautious in times of recession or high uncertainty and she is overly optimistic when the economy is booming and seems to be unstoppable. As a result, during "hard times" Janet, like other bankers, is more likely to reject projects that might have been successful and during "good times" Janet is more likely to approve projects that ultimately turn out to be unprofitable. This tendency amplifies similar changes in fear and confidence, which is exhibited in households and entrepreneurs and produces the boom and bust behavior of the economy.

Summary of the Banker

The financial sector in the United States economy is extensive and competitive. Households have an array of choices in where to save, and entrepreneurs have choices in where to seek investment funds. Banks, representing the financial sector, have the essential role of selecting which projects to finance. Using good lending practices and business judgment, the banker selects the projects she believes is most likely to be successful (at least successful enough to pay back the loan with interest). However, being human, bankers can be overly cautious in hard times and overly optimistic in good times.

THE POLITICIAN

The role of the politician is to protect people and property. To carry out this mission, politicians are invested by the people with authority and police power.

Politicians make and enforce rules that control the economy. The scope of control is vast. Examples include rules to protect safety in food, rules that dictate terms of employment, and rules that govern saving for retirement. With all these rules, some are bound to be ridiculous, such as rules that require a license to arrange flowers. Like many other examples in economics, more rules have diminishing value. The first rules are very useful. But as rules are layered on rules, their usefulness wanes, sometimes even to the point of being harmful.

Some politicians are elected. The elected politicians appoint other politicians to be regulators and staff. While regulators have power and use their power to issue rules and dictates, regulators follow the direction set by elected politicians. The politician in the PP&P model (below) is Sam, who represents the whole political class, including regulators, who make the rules.

Here is Sam, the PP&P model politician. Sam was President of Student Government in High School. He was a Political Science major before he went on to Law School. His first job was as a volunteer campaign worker for Representative Cabot. He later joined the congressional staff of Rep. Cabot, and eventually was elected to the House seat formerly held by now Senator Cabot. Sam loves politics.

Most government workers are not politicians; they are simply the part of the household-supplied labor force that does the work of providing government services. It is the top officials of the government apparatus who are politicians.

Motivation

In the PP&P model, politicians like Sam are assumed to be motivated by power and the urge to be in control. Politicians are usually well-educated, and perhaps even public-spirited. Sam considers himself to be a "public servant." Sam has strong opinions about how the economy should work and he is motivated to control the economy according to his views. Politicians carry out their vision through the apparatus of bureaucracy, enforced by police power.

The urge to control, to be in power, is bipartisan. Power needs limits to prevent tyranny. There are Constitutional limits to the power of politicians. However, the Constitution, after two hundred years of interpretation, is looking pretty tattered. The government is able to do many things that at first reading one might think are not allowed by the Constitution. Perhaps households could control politicians via the ballot box. In fact, this is a very weak means of controlling politicians. Voters are diffused and confused by the scope of issues. A particular household might be unhappy with the way Sam is protecting the poor (or not), or protecting the environment (or not), and at the same time is satisfied enough with the job he is doing in "bringing home the bacon" to Sam's district. (Anyway, that guy running against Sam may not be any different. Better the devil you know than the devil you don't know.)

In the PP&P model, the only effective limit on the power of politicians is their ability to extract money from the economy. Politicians derive power from their capability to spend money, and money comes from taxes. Money can also be borrowed, essentially borrowing power from future governments, spending taxes yet to be collected.

If households rebel against rising taxes, incumbent politicians risk losing power at the next election. But, as discussed earlier, this is a weak threat. The more significant constraint on politicians is that if they keep raising tax rates, they eventually reach the turning point where they cannot extract more revenue from households. Economist Art Laffer explained how this constraint works using the simple Laffer Curve shown below.

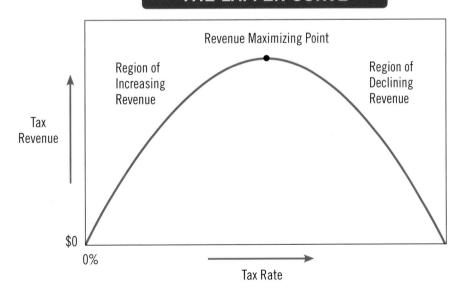

When tax rates are low, people do not bother to avoid paying tax. But as tax rates rise, taxpayers try harder to avoid the increasingly burdensome tax. They might shift their use of time to activities that are not taxed, or devise some other path to avoid taxes. At some point, the tax rate is so high, and taxpayers adjust their behavior so much, that the actual tax revenue collected decreases, as shown in the Laffer Curve graph on page 33. The PP&P model assumes that politicians raise taxes until they reach the Revenue Maximizing Point. That is the limit to their power.

The reader may object to the depiction of government officials as motivated by power and control, and rightly point out that not all politicians act like they are "anointed elites." Fair enough. The point is analogous to the caricature of business leaders. While most business leaders are not greedy, money-grubbing misanthropes, business leaders *are* motivated by profit. Politicians may not be megalomaniacal control freaks, but they *are* motivated by power and the conceit that they have a better vision for America.

Time

Time affects politicians too. Politicians are forward-looking, but they focus myopically on the next election. Such short-term thinking means that politicians may not give enough attention to longer-term problems. An example of political

myopia is twenty-plus years of inaction dealing with the long-term financing problems of Social Security and Medicare. Another problem with next-election myopia is the propensity of politicians to borrow and spend taxes yet to be collected by future governments. When the future gets here, those future politicians, who will have reduced power due to inherited debt, will not think kindly about those in control before them.

Summary of the Politician

The politician's job is to protect the people and property of the economy. The politician is invested with police power and authority. Therefore, government attracts people who are motivated by power, who have an urge to control. Power is exercised to maintain power and implement their agenda for how society should be structured. There is only weak institutional constraint on politicians through elections. The effective limit on the power of politicians is their inability to extract more tax revenue from households once the turning point of the Laffer Curve has been reached.

The Three Cycles of the Economy

This chapter explains how money flows through the economy in three cycles of the Production, Property & Power model. We present a simple, but plausible explanation of the forces at work in each of the cycles and how the three cycles interact with each other. The model generally is self-correcting. There is a natural balance among the various forces that affect the economics agents of the economy: the households, the entrepreneurs, bankers, and the government. When the economy is disturbed from its natural balance, the people of the economy act according to their perceptions and preferences to eventually find a new balance. The Production, Property & Power economy adjusts to each change as people pick themselves up and get back to doing what they do.

THE PRODUCTION CYCLE: Making and Getting

How does the economy produce the goods and services that households want and need? This is not a trivial question. The economy of the former Soviet Union, for example, was unable to produce what the people wanted. In the United States, we take it for granted that the market will provide whatever we want. And usually, we are right.

This happy outcome is not thanks to some benevolent economic czar, who knows what is best for us. That has been tried in socialist economies and every time it ends badly. The abundance we observe in the United States is the result of a "free-enough" economic system. Consumers are free enough to choose what they buy, and producers of goods and services are free enough to try to earn profits, which motivate them to adjust quickly and efficiently to produce what people want to buy. Adam Smith compared this amazing system to an "invisible hand" guiding the economy. Consumers and producers are motivated to pursue their own interests, yet both flourish by satisfying the wants of the other.

In the Production cycle, consumer goods firms produce goods and services wanted by households and capital goods firms produce equipment (aka capital goods) wanted by other firms. The Production cycle does not include government services (defense, justice, public works, public education, welfare, etc.). As we shall see, these services are provided in the Power cycle.

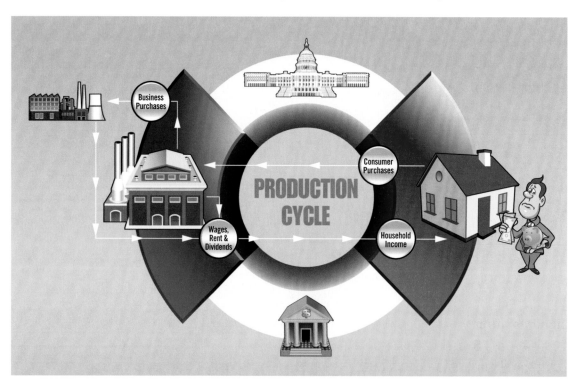

Figure 3.1: Flow of Money in the Production Cycle

The arrows in Figure 3.1 show the direction of the circular flow of money in the Production cycle. Firms produce goods and services. To produce the goods, they pay wages to workers, rents to use the factories, and equipment and firms pay interest and dividends to the providers of financial capital. Wages, rents, interest and dividends become income to households. Households use the income to purchase the goods and services, providing revenue to the consumer goods firms. The firms that make consumer goods buy equipment from other firms that make capital goods. Firms use these revenues to start the production cycle all over again, paying wages to workers and so on.

It must be emphasized that every money transfer is in exchange for a reciprocal transfer of services or material goods. Wages are exchanged for hours of labor. Interest and dividends are paid in exchange for the use of financial capital. Payments from the household to the firm are in exchange for goods or services from the firm. It is in the exchange that overall well-being is increased. The flow of money depicted in Figure 3.1 has a corresponding flow (not depicted) of activities in the opposite direction as the multitude of exchanges takes place.

One can imagine that the flows of money and the reciprocal flows of goods and services are pressurized by the intensity of human action, like a heart applying pressure to pump blood through a body. When people have a healthy outlook and are confident about their future, pressure in the Production cycle is strong and steady and times are good. When people become anxious, and worried about their future, the pressure drops and something bad could happen.

We now consider the components of the Production cycle in more depth.

Firms

Firms produce goods and services. Firms are motivated to earn profits, as discussed in Chapter 2, because profits are necessary to stay in business. Some firms produce goods and services for households ("consumer goods"), and other firms produce goods and services for businesses ("capital goods.")

There are many products and services, which can be produced in different ways. The firm hires workers, obtains equipment and other capital it needs by paying competitive wages, rents, and profits. A firm may have to adjust wages higher to attract more workers, or it may lower wages if there are more workers than needed. Similar adjustments are made to rents to obtain buildings, equipment, land, and whatever else the firm needs to produce goods and services.

Firms look to markets to find the workers and capital they need. The firm hires workers in labor markets, acquires the physical plant and equipment it needs in capital goods markets, buys raw materials in the commodities markets, and raises the money it needs in financial markets.

The firm sells its goods and services to specific consumers who want to buy that good or service. To find these specific customers, the firms bring their products and services to customized retail markets. For example, farmers sell their goods in grocery markets, Hollywood sells its services in movie theatres, and publishers sell books on Amazon. Finding the right market does not guarantee that sales transactions will occur. Firms have to make adjustments to their prices or product to be more competitive based on what they learn in the markets.

In the Production cycle, the choices made by a firm are simple: find the most profitable way to produce the goods. An important outcome is that firms cannot earn excess profits, that is, profits above the amount necessary to stay in business. Excess profits are a sign that another firm can produce the good more efficiently. If there are above-normal profits, they soon disappear as competition works its magic to eliminate excess profits. (The reader may wonder at this claim, since there are, in fact, very profitable companies. As we shall see, above-normal profits are a return on innovation and learning, not production.)

Households

Heads of households make the best decisions they can regarding how to spend household resources. In doing so, decision-makers must balance what is best for their current household as well as their future household. They spend their resources to achieve the best mix of utility from the enjoyment of consumption, now and in the future, and utility from a reduction of fear and anxiety, now and in the future.

In the Production cycle, there are two types of decisions facing the household. One set of decisions is about how the household should spend its income. Another set of decisions is about how the household should spend its time. Where should they work, and how much time should be spent at work? In the next section on the Property cycle, we will consider complex decisions about saving for the future. For now, we consider the Production cycle decisions about how to spend money and time.

Households buy goods and services from the firms. The head of household chooses from among a vast selection of consumer goods and services those

that are best for the household. In choosing, the decision-maker considers the price, quality, convenience, and whatever other factors are important to him or her. The choices of the household give information to the firms about what to produce, as described above. Household spending on goods and services becomes revenue to the firms, cycling through the Production cycle.

Households choose to supply labor to firms or not. Depending on many factors, such as wages, work conditions, job flexibility, and so on, households choose to sell their services in the labor market. If they are unable to find employment, they may accept a lower wage, or choose a different type of work, or make other adjustments until they find a firm willing to offer a job. They arrive at a wage, number of hours, intensity of effort, etc., that is mutually acceptable to the worker and the firm.

Households own the firms, either directly through shares, or indirectly, such as through a pension or mutual fund. Households also own all the non-public lands and natural resources, either directly or indirectly. Income earned by households comes from firms. They earn wages for their labor, rents for capital and land, sales revenues for natural resources, and dividends distributed by profit-making firms. This income drives the decision-making process for the household as the cycle continues again and again.

Equilibrium

When the forces that motivate firms and households do not cause any further adjustments in decisions, we say the economy is in equilibrium; everything is balanced. Obviously, equilibrium is only a theoretical concept, since wages, prices, rents, etc. are always being adjusted and new products and services are always being introduced. But it is a useful theoretical concept, nonetheless.

In the production economy, for example, equilibrium means that households are working the number of hours they want to work, at the wage being offered. It means their household income is enough to buy the goods and services they want. Their desire for more consumer goods is less than their desire for more leisure time. They choose not to work more hours to generate more income to buy more stuff. The tension between the desire to enjoy consumption is in balance with the desire to not work.

Equilibrium means that prices fully pay for the cost of production. Profits are enough that firms are not motivated to increase or cut production. Firms are making enough profit to keep from bankruptcy, but not so much profit that they wish to expand production or attract competiton. There is a tension in the system; the system is balanced and unchanged from period to period. An out of balance condition would disrupt equilibrium and set in motion adjustments to consumption and production, employment and capacity utilization, as firms seek to regain profitability and households seek to achieve their best outcome.

What is the difference between equilibrium and stagnation? Or, to put it more positively, how does a healthy economy grow, so that future households anticipate a rising standard of living, rather than the exact same life as the present household? The Production cycle has no answer to that question. In the Production cycle, firms and households adjust their decisions until production and consumption are in balance. Thereafter, nothing in the model would cause the economy to change. To explain the emergence of economic growth, we must add the Property cycle to the model.

THE PROPERTY CYCLE: From Stagnant Equilibrium to Vibrant Growth

The Production cycle is an efficient and stability-seeking environment of production and consumption, over and over, with no mechanism for change. By contrast, the Property cycle is a dynamic, unstable environment in which risk-taking entrepreneurs use on-again/off-again savings from households to develop innovations that have the potential to improve lives. Of course, not

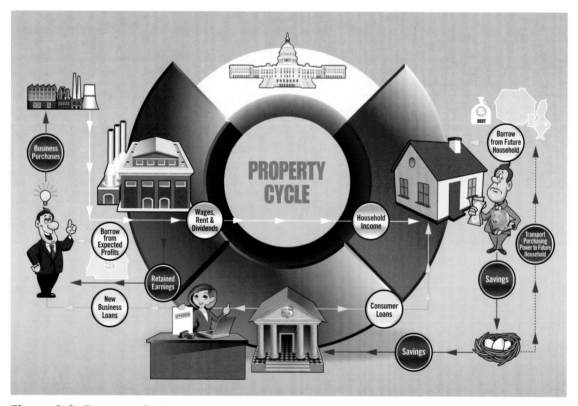

Figure 3.2: Property Cycle

every innovation is successful. But the outcome of innovations that succeeded over the last 300 years is impressive.

There are two halves to the Property Cycle: One half relates to the household decision to save for the future, and the other half deals with entrepreneurs who invest in business innovations. The two halves are joined together through separate connections to banks. To see how this works, "follow the money" through the Property Cycle.

Jack, the head of the household, decides to save some income in a "nest egg." He anticipates he will want to use that money at some time in the future. He puts his savings nest egg in the bank. The bank aggregates Jack's savings with savings from many other households to form a larger pool of depositors' money. Then the bank offers business loans to entrepreneurs, who plan to invest in a new business idea. Tom, for example, needs more funds than the company he works for, Acme, can provide out of retained earnings. So, Tom applied for a business loan to obtain the remaining financing. Janet, the loan officer at the bank, has just approved the business loan. Tom uses the loan to invest in new equipment he needs to develop his innovation from the capital goods factory. The capital goods factory uses the sales revenue to pay wages to its workers, to pay rent for the buildings and equipment, and pay dividends out of its profits. These payments become income for households, completing the Property Cycle.

(Dotted lines, such as those to and from the future household depicted as an outlined shadow, illustrate the transfer of purchasing power to and from the future, not present day cash flows.)

Jack could use his savings nest egg to acquire other forms of property (hence the name Property Cycle), either real assets or financial assets like the savings account used in this illustration. For simplicity, the PP&P model assumes Jack chooses to save his nest egg at the local bank. Other forms of property nest eggs eventually lead to the same outcome: purchasing power is stored for future use and funds are made available to entrepreneurs to develop new business investments. (If Jack chooses to hoard money in his mattress, the outcome is different; no funds are made available for entrepreneurs.)

Entrepreneurs are "Rock Stars"

Entrepreneurs are risk-taking people who, if they create successful market-tested innovations, increase profits (at least for a while) for their firms. Products that

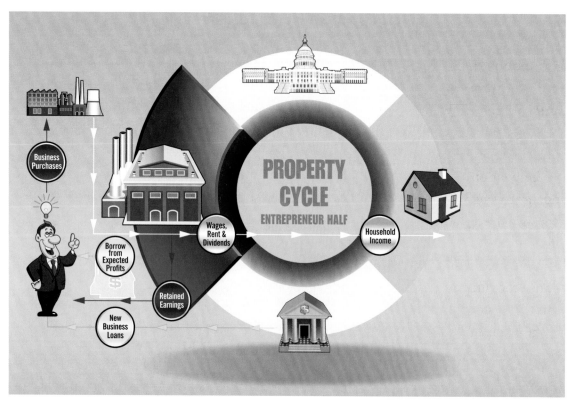

Figure 3.2.1 The Entrepreneur/Investment Half of the Property Cycle

become obsolete lose customers to the innovation. The Austrian economist Joseph A. Schumpeter called this process, "creative destruction." The new destroys the old.

Usually society gains more from an innovation than it loses, and sometimes society is much better off. Innovation breathes vitality into a stagnant economy and raises the standard of living. Firms that introduce successful innovations into the Production Cycle earn higher profits at first. Eventually, competition from imitators squeezes out the profits of innovators. As excess profits from innovation are eliminated, the Production Cycle equilibrium (stagnation?) is re-established, but at a higher standard of living than before the innovation.

You may wonder how a higher standard of living results from action in the Property cycle. When the entrepreneur's new product is finally ready for production, the household decision-maker, Jack, decides to buy the new product and do without other lower-valued goods. Factories that produce these low-value goods reduce production, laying off workers. Meanwhile, entrepreneurs and copy-cats are investing in new factories to produce the new product. This creates opportunities to hire the unemployed workers. (The employment transition takes time and is a serious practical problem in the process of creative destruction.) The evolution of the telephone illustrates the process of creative destruction, both the turmoil and the higher standard of living that emerges from the process. Landline telephones were made obsolete by cell phones, and cell phones were later made obsolete by smartphones. At one point in the 1970s, a million people were employed by the old telephone company. Many of these workers had to find new jobs in the changing economy.

Innovation arises spontaneously, but not randomly. Innovation is spontaneous; the eureka moment can happen unexpectedly. Innovation is not random because the entrepreneur is actively searching for such moments. The entrepreneur is the "rock star" of the free economy: the innovator, the discoverer. A few entrepreneurs do become famous, such as Steve Jobs or Elon Musk, but most entrepreneurs are ordinary people. Yet, it is the success of entrepreneurs that raises the standard of living.

In order to realize the potential of entrepreneurs, there must be resources available to invest in their ideas. In a free economy, these resources come from savings—either saving by firms, called retained earnings, or the savings of households.

Household Savings in the Property Cycle

Savings are necessary for the economy to grow and to provide resources for entrepreneurs to bring innovations to fruition. The Production Cycle has no mechanism for this change, which takes place in the Property cycle. The decision to save or not balances the enjoyment of consumption today, the expected enjoyment of consumption in the future, and a desire to avoid the anxiety of an insecure future. The "right" choice of savings is much more nuanced than is usually imagined.

Let's consider the choice facing Jack, the head of the household. Should the household spend more now or increase the family nest egg? For now, assume Jack's decision is based solely on the enjoyment of consumption; that is, Jack is choosing between enjoyment of consumption now or the anticipation of consumption in the future, say in retirement.

As humans, we know that enjoyment of a good usually diminishes as the quantity of consumption increases. Economists call this phenomenon "the law of diminishing marginal utility." One scoop of ice cream is delightful, five scoops is not five times as delightful. This common experience is why we like

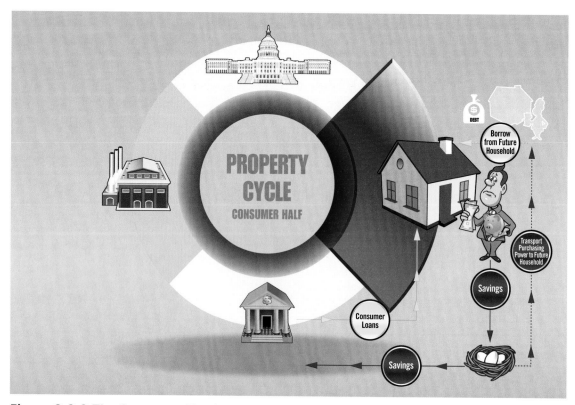

Figure 3.2.2 The Consumer/Savings Half of the Property Cycle

variety in life. "Variety is the spice of life." Each time we add a different experience in life we start the enjoyment process anew.

Jack probably does not realize it, but as he decides between more spending or more savings he is mentally comparing decreasing enjoyment from more consumption now to anticipated enjoyment of more consumption in the future. As Jack spends more and more on things today, Jack's enjoyment from more stuff now diminishes until it falls below the anticipated enjoyment of more stuff in retirement. At this point, Jack chooses to save more, not spend more.

Each household arrives at its own decision point. Some choose to emphasize stuff now, some emphasize stuff later. In some households the desire/need for stuff now is so strong that they transfer purchasing power from future households to spend in the present. This transfer is easily accomplished by borrowing against the credit card, creating a debt to be repaid in the future. Such "negative savings" reduces the net amount of funds available for business loans. The total net savings of all the households determines the amount of money available for banks to lend to entrepreneurs.

Interest Rates in the Savings Decision

When Jack makes his decision to save (or not) he considers the interest rate he will earn on savings. A low interest rate means Jack will anticipate a poorer outcome from his savings than if there were a high interest rate. (Remember, there is no inflation in the PP&P model. The level of interest rates in the PP&P model is not related to inflation, only to market forces for investment funds.) How would Jack's decision change if interest rates were higher or lower?

Suppose interest rates move higher. It then takes less savings to achieve the same level of future consumption than before interest rates increased. You might say that future consumption is "on sale." When something is on sale, we often buy more of it. The decision-maker may choose to increase savings to take advantage of higher interest rates and enjoy even greater consumption in the future.

But it's not that simple. Remember the law of diminishing marginal utility? As Jack anticipates a bigger nest egg in the future (due to higher interest rates), his expected enjoyment of incrementally larger future wealth diminishes. The enjoyment of additional spending today might be more satisfying than a lower level of enjoyment from more wealth in the future. The fact that future consumption is "on sale" allows Jack to save enough today to anticipate an acceptable level of enjoyment in the future and still have resources leftover to increase consumption today. Jack might choose to save more since future spending is "on sale," or he might choose to save less because higher returns will let him reach his goals with less saving.

The outcome of "the sale" depends on the personal preferences of the decision-maker. What we observe over many households is that there is a mix of some increased savings to take advantage of higher interest rates and some increased spending to balance the diminishing enjoyment of greater future consumption.

The same analysis applies in reverse when interest rates fall. Low interest rates make future consumption more expensive in that it takes more savings today to achieve a desired level of future consumption. Jack might want to "buy" less future consumption since the "price" is higher. However, the law of diminishing marginal utility also works in reverse. The last increment of future consumption (in a poorer future) provides greater utility than when the future was expected to be richer. The anticipation of greater incremental utility in the future may cause Jack to save a little more today, even with lower interest rates. In this way, Jack brings the expected enjoyment of future consumption in balance with the enjoyment of stuff today.

As was said earlier, the savings decision is complicated. But the story is about to get even more complicated.

Not Only Consumption, but also Security

Generally, people would rather have a stable lifestyle than a "feast or famine" type of existence. Households smooth out the ups and downs in their income by making adjustments to savings; when income is temporarily low, households spend more than they earn, and when income is temporarily high, they save more than usual. If Jack loses his job for some reason and he wants to maintain the same level of spending, he must consume some of the family savings from the past, or he must borrow from family income expected in the future. Jack chooses the pattern of consumption and saving that best fits the household (current and future). For example, if Jack believes the loss of a job is a short-term set-back, then he may borrow from expected future income to maintain the enjoyment of consumption today. But if he believes the job loss is a severe disruption to the security of the family, he is likely to use up some savings (sell property) and adjust present and future plans to a new reality. If Jack has a big nest egg, the lifestyle disruption is less traumatic.

The Property Nest Egg: Wealth Transport through Time

A household with a savings nest egg enjoys a sense of security; the bigger the nest egg, the greater is the sense of security. Property in the nest egg stores wealth (purchasing power) and makes it available to the future household. In other words, property is the mechanism to transport purchasing power through time.

Households save to smooth out the enjoyment of consumption over time. More importantly, however, people save to reduce fear and anxiety about an  uncertain future. Owning property provides security; the more property a household owns, the greater its feeling of security. The head of household, Jack, must achieve a balance between using the family resources to enjoy consumption now or saving more to enjoy consumption in the future and importantly, reduce anxiety about the future. When reducing fear is more satisfying than spending more on consumption, households will increase savings. When the enjoyment of more spending now is more satisfying than the security provided by owning more property, Jack will spend more and save less. As usual, there is a diminishing marginal effect from owning more property; the incremental security from more and more property eventually diminishes.

Smoothing out the enjoyment of consumption over one's lifetime is one explanation for why households save. But a more convincing explanation for why people save is to reduce anxiety by preparing for an unknown future with a larger nest egg. That explanation relates to both the emotional part of our nature and the rational side of humanity. Evidence for the effect of anxiety on saving decisions is the fact that the personal savings rate in the United States dropped when Social Security was introduced in 1937, and it dropped again when Medicare was introduced in 1964. As people increased their reliance on government for personal financial security, they reduced the self-reliance of a household nest egg.

The Importance of Property and Property Rights to the Economy and Society

The owner of Property has stored wealth, which gives the owner freedom of action in the future. The right to own property is fundamental to freedom and to a free economy. Property rights empower incentives, which unleash the creative human spirit to breathe life into an economy. Property rights enable property to operate as a nest egg, to effectively transfer wealth forward to future households and thereby reduce insecurity in the present household. Without property rights, households are unable to provide security for their future through savings. Without savings, the entrepreneur loses a key source of finance for innovation. Without innovation, the economy becomes stagnant and people live needlessly impoverished lives.

Property rights are not only critical to a free economy, they are fundamental for a society of free and independent people. Without property rights, the people must rely on the tender mercies of government for security through taxation and social welfare programs. Without savings, entrepreneurs depend on lobbyists to be their champion for politically motivated government investments. Without property rights, the individual is made feeble and the central government empowered.

Volatility

The urge to reduce fear and anxiety is a volatile force. In contrast, the urge to consume appears to be a stable force, even allowing for the occasional binge. But fear can spike up suddenly in response to an economic event such as a layoff or a major hurricane. The household decision-maker reassesses earlier choices and makes a new allocation of family resources. If there are no further shocks, then fear subsides and a "normal" level of anxiety is restored. The household

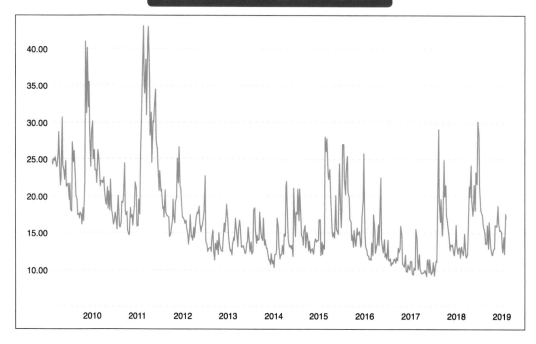

CHART VIX: "FEAR INDEX"

restores the earlier set of choices. This pattern of spikes in fear and gradual return to normal is on display in stock prices, for example, and is observed in the pattern of prices for the VIX, the so-called "fear-index."

When fear spikes, households will focus on reducing fear rather than the enjoyment of more consumption. Households will be driven to build a bigger nest egg. Spending that is the least rewarding will be cut back to allow for increased savings. Over time, as fear subsides, the urge to reduce fear will fade, and households will return to their usual pattern of spending and saving. Passage of time is a natural antidote to fear-driven spikes in savings behavior. Unfortunately, the household reaction to a spike in fear can itself cause new problems in the economy, as we will discuss later with regard to the business cycle.

When fear strikes, the household with a property nest egg has options; it can sell property to meet current needs. Property itself generates utility in that it gives the household more options, smoothing out reactions, and reduces the intensity of fear-driven spikes of saving. The household without property has fewer options. The ability to borrow from a future household is limited.

In households where income is "lumpy" and disruptions are common (e.g., commission-based compensation), the decision-maker will try to accumulate savings to see them through frequent disruptions to income. In households with stable and secure income, there is less motivation to accumulate a nest egg.

The Paradox of Savings

Understanding the fear-driven savings pattern, the great twentieth century economist, John Maynard Keynes, famously popularized "the paradox of savings." The idea is that households respond to economic bad times with a fear-driven spike in savings. As fear causes households to cut back spending, firms will be forced to reduce production and lay off workers. The worst fears of households are then realized. Keynes mis-identified the blame for this state-of-affairs as *over-saving*, and condemned saving. (Keynes lived during the gold standard era, when hoarding gold was possible. Hoarding gold is saving that does not empower business investment. That type of saving is harmful.) But in general, it is more valid to put the blame on under-investing, not over-saving. Keynes correctly urged more public works to counter under-investing. Nonetheless, his misplaced animus against saving still echoes today.

After Keynes, public policy no longer encouraged saving and instead consumption became a public virtue; exactly the opposite of common sense. Policymakers before Keynes encouraged citizens to be thrifty and productive. Policymakers after Keynes needed little persuasion to borrow and increase government spending. Developed countries are heavily indebted from a misguided "spending is good" Keynesian mindset. Many countries, including the United States, have government budgets that are burdened by debt inherited from past governments. Mis-applied arguments against saving mean that eighty years after Keynes we have accumulated public debt instead of accumulated capital and household wealth.

Banks in the Property Cycle: Mind the Gap

So far, we have discussed entrepreneurs, who need funds to develop innovation and households, who accumulate nest eggs. The bank closes the gap between the household, which supplies funds through savings, and the entrepreneur who invests the funds in new developments. The bank satisfies both parties.

In the PP&P model, entrepreneurs can obtain funds from two sources. One source is a bank, which aggregates household savings and another source is from the savings of firms, aka retained earnings. Much business investment in the United States comes from retained earnings. But a very significant amount is financed by banks (or other financial institutions).

Entrepreneurs compete to obtain credit from the bank based on the available pool of savings. The banker (Janet, from chapter 2) evaluates loan applications from entrepreneurs and selects the projects she believes will be most profitable

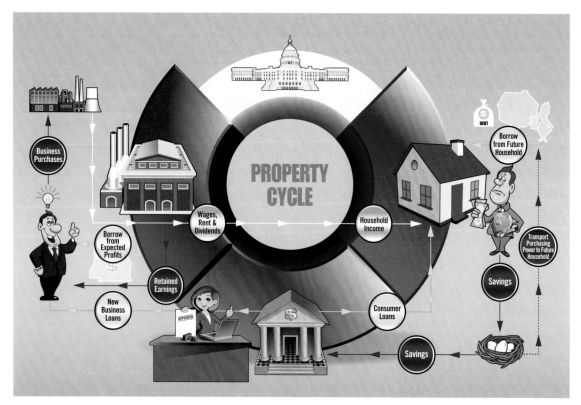

Figure 3.2.3 The Banker in the Property Cycle

to the bank and rejects the others. Most profitable to the bank does not guarantee funding for the "best" projects for society. There is an expected strong correlation between the projects most desirable to bankers and the projects with the greatest value to society. (This is clearly not always the case. For example, over-financing of home-building led to the financial crisis of 2008.)

Free market forces work to direct choices to the "best" outcome. For example, Tom, the entrepreneur for Acme, is so confident of the success of his project, he is willing to agree to a higher interest rate to get the money he needs. Two years ago, he decided against going ahead with a project because the interest

rate required by the bank was too high. His project back then was quite risky, and Tom was unsure Acme could make a profit at such a high cost of financing. This time he is gung-ho for development.

Some entrepreneurial ideas are too risky for banks to finance. These ideas must find a wealthy risk-loving patron like Jeff Bezos,

CEO of Amazon and Blue Origin, or a wealthy and politically sympathetic Uncle Sam.

The bank closes the gap between the household and the entrepreneur. Jack deposits the household savings at the bank. Janet, the banker, evaluates various loan applications and approves Tom's entrepreneurial project for a new business loan. Tom uses the money to invest in new capital (i.e., factories, equipment, processes, etc.). The spending for new capital at the capital goods factory generates wages, rents, and profits, which become income to households like Jack's. The Property Cycle is completed. See Figure 3.2.

Equilibrium in the Property Cycle

Equilibrium, i.e., balance, in the Property Cycle, is when the amount of funds wanted by entrepreneurs is equal to the amount of money available from retained earnings plus the amount of money available through banks from household savings.

Free market forces act in financial markets to maintain this balance through adjustments to interest rates. If funds are in short supply, Tom, who really wants the money, offers to pay a higher interest rate for the loan. This leads to higher interest rates for all other borrowers. Higher interest rates cause some entrepreneurs to cancel their plans, which reduces the total funds needed until it equals the total funds available. Since the bank is earning a higher interest rate on the loan, it is willing to pay more interest to attract more savings. Jack decides to save more because of the attractive interest rates. At the higher interest rates, more funds are supplied and fewer entrepreneurs want funding. (The same outcome is achieved if a higher interest rate convinces Jack to stop using his credit card. In this case, the money that Jack does not spend on his credit card is available to lend to entrepreneurs.). The shortage of funds evaporates; balance is restored. Note that the reason rates go higher is the enthusiasm of the entrepreneur for the success of the investment. High interest rates will be attractive to only the most convinced entrepreneurs who believe in their idea.

On the other hand, if Janet has more funds to loan than good projects to finance, Janet will offer to lend at a lower interest rate. This action would attract loan applications from hesitant entrepreneurs (increasing the demand for loans) and make saving less attractive to households (reducing the supply of available credit). More demand and less supply, and soon Janet's funds are no longer in excess. Balance is achieved.

Entrepreneurs like Tom are forward-looking risk-takers, evaluating the prospects for profitable new business investments. When business conditions are good and Tom can clearly "see" profitable possibilities, he becomes more confident and eager for money to make new business investments. Tom's confidence, and the confidence of others like him, pushes interest rates higher. But when business conditions are not good and there is limited "visibility" into the future, Tom becomes cautious and waits for a clearer outlook. Their caution reduces demand for business loans. Banks respond by lowering interest rates to stir up more demand for loans.

The balance maintained by market adjustments in interest rates is an uneasy equilibrium. Tom's business confidence can change quickly in response to economic events. Households like Jack's are subject to changing degrees of fear and anxiety, which affect how much they save. Bankers like Janet are people too, and they are affected by more than just spreadsheets. In periods of a strong economy, Janet can become over-confident and approve even quite risky loans. But in bad times, Janet becomes more cautious and approves only the projects that are almost certain to succeed. It is remarkable how the free market system balances the disparate influences and motivations of households, entrepreneurs, and bankers. Sometimes it fails, at least for a while.

Trouble in Equilibrium Paradise: The Business Cycle

If Jack (and other households) experiences a sudden anxiety spike, perhaps due to a plant closure in a nearby town, there could soon be trouble in the economy. Jack cuts back unnecessary spending to increase savings and build up his nest egg more quickly, thereby reducing his feeling of insecurity. A bigger supply of savings causes banks to lower interest rates to slow the growth of savings and increase demand for business loans. But lower interest rates do not always increase demand for investment funds, especially when Tom (and other entrepreneurs) is unsure about the health of the economy. Janet (the banker) cannot find enough projects to approve. In this uncertain economy, Janet is satisfied to let the savings go unused for a while, until things settle down.

Jack is not the only household spooked into cutting back unnecessary spending. A rapid drop in consumer spending by many households results in lower production and layoffs. In good times, entrepreneurs would invest and hire workers to develop their investments. But in this time of high anxiety the surge in household savings is not being used for new investments. Idled production resources are not re-employed. There is potential for a vicious cycle of fear leading to reduced consumption and more unused savings, and so on.

Bankers like Janet are motivated by profit-making opportunities. But the presence of fear and uncertainty in the economy may affect their calculation of expected future profits and may inject an extra measure of caution as they evaluate loan applications. Keynes referred to this tendency as "animal spirits." The idea is captured in the metaphor of bulls and bears in the financial markets of Wall Street, for example.

The same fear that causes Jack to increase savings will also cause Tom to reduce his demand for new savings, at the very same time. Tom realizes that his project may not be successful in an uncertain economy. The increased supply of savings sits idle. The business cycle gets underway as the economy heads into recession. (See Appendix A for an extended discussion of business cycles.)

As mentioned earlier, time is the antidote to fear. Eventually, a new equilibrium starts to form in the economy. Prices fall, which motivates Jack to increase purchases at the lower prices. Tom senses the turn in the economy, and takes advantage of low interest rates to start some business investments. Janet is concerned that the idle savings is costing her bank profit and works harder to make new loans. The business cycle turns favorable and businesses start to hire and expand again. New business investment leads to more employment, which leads to more income, which leads to lower fear, greater consumption, more production, and so on. The business cycle enters the boom phase.

The Property cycle is the battleground where policymakers fight recession. During the Depression, Keynes, and many other economists, called on government to increase public works. While most economists argued for public works for humanitarian relief reasons, Keynes argued that a timely increase in public investment would put idle savings to work, keep workers usefully employed, and restore business confidence.

The Rise of the Power Economy

Politicians loved the new ideas of Keynes. It gave them an intellectual argument to expand control of the economy. The pesky old-school economists were generally against government intervention. But the misery of the Great Depression and the new Keynesian concepts opened the door for politicians to take control of the economy. Western economies have never looked back...yet.

The Production, Property & Power model of the economy is more complex than the old circular flow model that is standard in all Introductory Economics textbooks. The Property Cycle of the model introduces essential elements of forward-looking decision-makers with human motivations, property in which forward-looking households can store value, and risk-taking bankers and entrepreneurs who drive innovation and economic growth.

There is still one more sector of the PP&P model that is vital to understanding the modern economy. That is the role of government in the economy. For that we turn to the Power cycle.

THE POWER CYCLE: Intervention on Purpose

Government accounts for more than 40% of GDP (Gross Domestic Product—a measure of a nation's economic activity), not even counting the enormous amounts of income redistributed by the government. Government controls the rest of the economy through regulations. Government economic activity cannot be ignored in a meaningful model of the economy. Thus, the Power Cycle integrates government activity into the Production, Property & Power model.

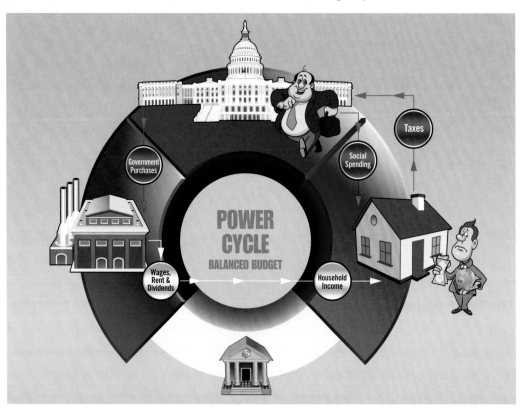

Figure 3.3.1 The Power Cycle (Balanced Budget)

Follow the Money

As in the rest of the PP&P model, economic agents are people…with human behavior. In the Power cycle, decision-makers are the top government officials: the elected and appointed politicians, the ones who control power. They are "government controllers" as much as they are "public servants." Even in every-day usage, the media refers to certain top officials as "czars," as in "energy czar" or "drug czar."

As explained in Chapter 2, the PP&P model assumes politicians are moti-vated by power and an urge to control. Power and control are made possible through money that is obtained by taxing the economic potential of the econ-omy. (Remember, only people pay taxes). Once politicians have control of tax revenues, they spend according to their political agenda.

The first rule of exercising power is to stay in power. So, politicians spend tax money in the way they think is most likely to keep them in power. Some spending will go to firms to acquire goods and services to carry out their gov-ernment duties. Some is spent to provide social services to households, such as welfare spending or spending for public schools. As can be seen in Figure 3.3.1, government spending ultimately flows back to households, although not the same households from whence came taxes. The Power cycle (balanced budget version) is complete.

Equilibrium in the Power Cycle

Equilibrium in the Power cycle is when the politicians' urge to control is constrained by the unwillingness of the people to pay more taxes. The ultimate constraint on the power of politicians is tax avoidance behavior, depicted in the Laffer Curve (See Chapter 2.4). Politicians are motivated to keep raising tax rates until further efforts to increase tax rates are counter-productive, and would reduce total tax revenue; i.e., the downward slope portion of the Laffer Curve.

Politicians also exercise power and control by making rules and regulations as well as through taxing and spending. Of course, without the power of tax-ation, rules and regulations are unenforceable. Initially, regulation has enor-mous value to the economy, bringing order and standards, which save lives and money. For example, painted lines and "keep to the right" rules on the highway keep cars in their lanes. Regulations which require banks to maintain minimum levels of cash and reserves enhance public confidence in the financial system and help it to work more smoothly. Like many other aspects of the economy, however, the value of additional regulation diminishes as more and more rules are piled up on each other. As companies face more and more regulations, with diminishing value and increasing cost, they are motivated to relocate the business to less regulated countries. In effect, there is a Laffer Curve effect with regulation as well as with taxation. The whole topic of regulation and its effect on the economy is beyond the scope of the Production, Property & Power model. We simply assume that regulation is part of the control responsibilities of government, with no analysis of its value.

Politicians like Sam, the face of politicians in the PP&P model, provide government services in exchange for taxes collected. Unlike the Production Cycle or the Property Cycle, exchange in the Power Cycle is not voluntary; the taxpayer does not negotiate a tax he or she is willing to pay, nor can he or she refuse to pay their tax, even if they don't want more government services. Sam and his political allies set the tax rate and enforce compliance through police power.

Not surprisingly, when households have no choice but to pay the tax, Sam's government services are not delivered with the attention to quality or customer care that Jack's household routinely expects from firms that provide consumer goods. Again, not surprisingly, government services often come at a high cost. There is no profit motive to control cost, no competition to discipline the inefficient, and no mechanism to reliably eliminate unnecessary or obsolete services. While Sam's government does deliver services, even valuable and necessary services, it often does so with room for improvement.

The range of services provided by government has grown over the years. Initially, government focused on protecting the lives and property of its citizens. However, politicians discovered the value that people like Jack place on reducing insecurity. This has greatly expanded the scope of possible government services to virtually the whole economy.

Do Sam and the government that he is part of produce valuable services? Yes. The core level of services provided by government are highly valuable to households and firms. Sam's primary mission is still to protect citizens from external and internal evil forces. Sam also provides a social safety net that reduces anxiety of unfortunate events, like unemployment or disability. Sam protects citizens from unscrupulous actors, who would pollute or cheat in pursuit of undeserved profit. Core government services are so valuable, in fact, that Jack, and other households, tolerate the waste and petty corruption they know frequently accompanies government services.

Political Control of the Economy

Sam and his colleagues in Congress grant themselves power to control parts of the economy. Gradually, year by year, legislative act by legislative act, Sam extends the reach of government into the economy.

Expanding power follows a common path. A devastating event or scandal occurs. People are shocked, perhaps with hype from the media. Sam promises action to protect against this outrage, if only he had more power and control. Examples of this well-trodden path to greater power are rampant. *The Jungle*, by Upton Sinclair, set up the Food and Drug Administration. The bankruptcy of Studebaker resulted in public support for government control of pensions. More recently, the financial crisis in 2008 led to the Dodd-Frank Act which expanded government control over the financial system. As Rahm Emanuel, then chief of staff for President Obama, clearly explained, "You never want a serious crisis to go to waste. And what I mean by that is an opportunity to do things you think you could not do before."

When a shock causes fear and uncertainty to spike, households want to reduce fear and uncertainty. For a little while, the public is willing to pay a higher price in taxes and loss of freedom than they would be willing to pay once fear had subsided. This creates a window of opportunity for politicians to expand control, when the public is less sensitive to price and more sensitive to assuaging fear. Once the expansion of control is in place, and the cost that goes with it, it is difficult to dismantle.

Since 1900, government has become a greater influence in decisions by households about savings and investment (the Property Cycle). The progressive income tax and Social Security both came into being in the first half of the twentieth century. The progressive income tax made it more difficult for households to build a nest egg. The tax took away from households exactly the portion of income which might have been available for savings. Social Security reduced fear of poverty in old age, a major motivation to build a nest egg. People like Jack decided they did not need to save to support themselves in old age. They paid taxes for Social Security. They did not feel anxiety despite a lack of savings, since they believe Sam's promise that Social Security will be there for them in their old age. And they don't have any extra money to save anyway, after paying their Social Security and progressive income taxes.

In the 1960s, Congress extended control of the economy with Medicare and new welfare programs. There is now even less motivation for households to save and less money available to save after taxes; Jack further reduced the household savings rate and increased the portion of disposable income spent for consumer goods. Currently on the political horizon there is growing interest in government-provided college and other "free" stuff. Still more reason to cut back savings (and pay higher taxes).

Jack is grateful for reduced fear and insecurity in facing an uncertain future. Sam knows that fear is a powerful motivator. Sam's challenge is to persuade enough people that more government control (and correspondingly higher taxes) will reduce fear and insecurity so household decision-makers like Jack will overcome their resistance to higher taxes. Sam has to make sure that reduced anxiety from more government control is greater than the increased anxiety from higher taxes and less after-tax income.

Jack is especially willing to support more government control if Sam promises to tax some other household, like Sean on the rich side of town. This important element in the politics of democracies is beyond the scope of the PP&P model. Nonetheless, in the long run, the ultimate economic constraint on politicians remains the Laffer Curve—the willingness of taxpayers to eventually change their economic activity to avoid excessive taxation.

Let's be optimistic that as the Laffer Curve constrains politicians, Sam and his friends pay more attention to quality and value of government services. Perhaps obsolete government services or rules that do the least public good may be eliminated by Sam himself, to repurpose scarce tax revenues to a higher value. This optimistic hope might be happening already, but for a big, one-time only, loophole.

Deficits and Debt

Politicians are not restricted to raising money only through taxation. Sam (and political friends in Congress) borrow money to spend, based on the credit-worthiness of future governments to pay the cost of the debt. In the years since the 1960 election of President Kennedy, the first President to embrace Keynesian economic policies, the United States government spent more money than it collected in taxes in every year but five. These annual budget deficits are financed by borrowing from the taxing ability of future governments, adding to the national debt. The United States government is therefore heavily indebted. Not even accounting for the unfunded promises of Social Security and Medicare, the national debt is now $66,866 for every man, woman and child living in the United States. How are we to understand this facet of the economy?

When politicians borrow and spend, they are usurping power that rightly belongs to future politicians. To pay the cost of accumulated debt, future politicians will have to use taxes they collect in the future to pay for past borrowing. Future households will pay taxes for which they will not receive any government services. This situation already exists in some cities and some states that are heavily burdened by past debt. Current residents pay high taxes, but after paying the cost of debt (including unfunded pension promises), there is not enough revenue leftover to provide the full range of government services expected by the people. The Laffer curve comes into play and residents flee the city or state to avoid high taxes. Examples of states with this problem are New Jersey, Connecticut and Illinois. This scenario is also starting to affect the national government, as the reality of the cost of unfunded Social Security, Medicare and accumulated debt impact the ability of politicians to enact their agendas. Future politicians will have less power, thanks to debt incurred by past and present politicians.

In the short run, borrowing is an easier path for politicians to get money (and power) than to tax current taxpayers. The Constitution places the authority to tax and to borrow with Congress and particularly the House of Representatives, which faces voters every two years. But in the short term, the Constitutional limitation on borrowing has not been an effective limitation on government to protect future governments from spendthrift politicians like Sam.

Borrow and burden future governments is not a path for unlimited government growth, however. Household decision-makers like Jack are concerned for the welfare of future households. They know that debt, whether private or public, reduces living standards of future households. Jack experiences increased anxiety for his future household, brought about by rising debt, public or private.

Jack does not clearly perceive the burden on his future household from government debt, due to the complexity of the progressive tax system and the inherent unknown nature of the future. Therefore Sam is able to borrow more than he otherwise could if each household's share of the future tax burden were more clearly known.

As the burden of government debt becomes significant, tax rates will increase. The Laffer Curve will make it more difficult for future governments to collect tax revenue. It will become more expensive for politicians to borrow money from wary lenders. Deficit financing will ultimately break down, as happened in recent years in developed economies: Greece, Spain, Portugal, Italy and Ireland. Borrowing is a big loophole to the Laffer Curve, but it is not unlimited.

Debt Loop(hole) in the Power Cycle

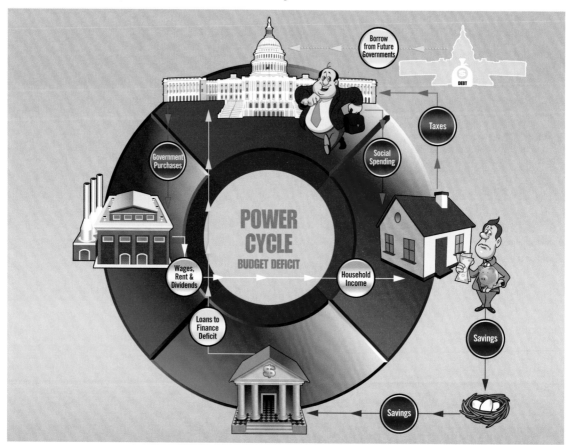

Figure 3.3.2 The Power Cycle with Deficit Spending

Figure 3.3.2 shows the Power Cycle with deficit borrowing and spending. Government borrowing diverts Jack's household savings away from financing entrepreneurs and towards financing Sam and other government politicians, who spend the money on their agenda.

We consider two possible situations: when there are idle savings and when there are no idle savings.

IDLE SAVINGS: Suppose a fear-inducing recession causes households to increase their savings and entrepreneurs to simultaneously decrease their demand for investment funds. In this case, banks are left with excess savings they are unable to lend. These idle savings can be borrowed by government for useful purposes such as new bridges or highways (or not so useful purposes like "cash for clunkers"). Either way, idle savings are put to work in the production cycle, raising employment, sales, and so on. The economy, which is in recession with unemployed workers and underutilized factories, is pushed in the direction of recovery.

This is classic Keynesian policy. Politicians could spend money on political projects that earn a positive return. Examples of such spending would be useful infrastructure or job retraining programs. Such projects grow the productive capacity of the economy, making the future burden of the debt more manageable. If politicians spend money in ways that do not earn a return, the full burden of debt falls on future governments. In a recession, there is much suffering in society from the effects of unemployment. The political urge to borrow and spend on social programs to alleviate suffering is understandably very strong. Therefore much of the spending to fight recession with borrowed money is spent on social spending without a future return.

NO IDLE SAVINGS: If the economy is not in recession, there is no large amount of idle savings. No matter. Politicians still want to spend more than what is collected in taxes to implement their "vision" of what America needs. When they do, politicians like Sam divert savings that would have been used by entrepreneurs to make new business investments. Interest rates increase as entrepreneurs compete for the pool of savings that is available. At higher interest rates, some innovation plans are no longer profitable, so they are cancelled, freeing up more funds for the government to borrow. This phenomenon is known as "crowding out" private investment.

The same concern about earning a return on government spending applies here as in the recession scenario above. It is even more significant in the situation without idle savings, however, since government spending is "crowding out" projects that could grow the economy and help future governments and future households. If the government borrows funds from other countries, there would be less crowding out of business investment. However, such government borrowing from other countries "crowds out" exports, since foreigners are choosing to lend money to the government instead of buying goods and services from American producers. In either case, "crowding out" investment in capital goods or "crowding out" exports, there is less production in the private sector of the economy, in favor of increased government spending.

Summary of the Power Economy

Politicians are motivated by power, and the urge to run the economy the way they think it should be run. They are enabled by taxes, which often expand after a crisis. Politicians habitually borrow to supplement tax revenues. Government taxing and borrowing takes savings out of the Property Cycle and redirects the money into the Power Cycle, either as government purchases of goods and services, or as social spending. Government debt involves a shift of purchasing power from a future government to the present government. Government policies with respect to taxation and social spending affect the decisions of households regarding savings and work. Government policies with respect to deficit financing affect interest rates and therefore decisions of households (savings) and entrepreneurs (business investment).

CONCLUSION

Figure 3.4 shows the PP&P model with all three cycles in one picture. The complete Production, Property & Power model consists of three inter-connected cycles: The Production Cycle in which workers and firms produce and consume goods and services; the Property Cycle in which household savings are collected in banks which make loans to entrepreneurs who spend the money on capital goods to develop innovations; and the Power Cycle, in which politicians carry out their political agendas, financed by tax revenues extracted from the economy and by borrowing against the taxing power of future governments.

Each of these cycles has its own dynamic that nudges decision-makers to a balance of forces. In the Production Cycle, prices of goods and services balance the firm's desire for profit against the buyer's assessment of getting their money's worth. Wages balance the firm's desire for workers against the worker's assessment of the value of time spent doing other activities. In the Property Cycle, the household balances enjoyment of spending on current consumption against saving up a nest egg to reduce the anxiety of an unknown future and to increase the potential enjoyment of consumption in the future. The banker weighs the return available from lending to an entrepreneur against the riskiness of the prospective project and the creditworthiness of the entrepreneur. The entrepreneur balances the likelihood of success from an innovation against the cost of funds to develop that innovation. In the Power cycle, the politician, motivated to "do good," balances an urge to raise taxes against the decreasing effectiveness of higher tax rates to increase revenues as taxpayers act to avoid

Figure 3.4 The Production, Property & Power Model

paying the tax (Laffer Curve behavior). A weak constraining force is the potential for a taxpayer revolt in the next election.

The PP&P model is obviously a highly simplified account of the actual economy. Just one of many omissions from the PP&P model is inter-connection of the economy with the rest of the world. The United States trades with most countries around the world, including global investment activities. As mentioned earlier, the PP&P model does not address monetary policy. The point is simply this: The PP&P model is merely a mental framework that provides a good starting place to understand how the economy works. The whole economy is the community of these inter-connected decision-makers, each acting according to the forces that motivate them. As they adjust to constantly changing situations over time, they act in ways that restore balance in the economy.

However, the economy is never in complete balance or equilibrium. The economy is always responding to events that disrupt the status quo. There may be temporary setbacks due to major shocks, such as hurricanes, geo-political events, or recessions. Households, entrepreneurs, bankers, and politicians constantly make their best adjustments, which moves the economy towards an elusive equilibrium. This consistent process of adjustment is itself a kind of balance and equilibrium, and produces an order of sorts to the economy. An ethical community of effective institutions and free decision-makers is a meta-equilibrium for a healthy economy in which individuals are free to live, to plan, to create; in a word, to flourish.

Appendix A

The Business Cycle

T he business cycle refers to the tendency of the economy to alternately go through periods of growth followed by recession. Economists in the modern era have tried to find an explanation for the business cycle. Two of the more enduring theories of the business cycle are from Frederick A. Hayek and John Maynard Keynes.

(Frederick A. Hayek was a prominent 20th century economist and a leading theorist of the "Austrian school." In this context, "Austrian" refers to a way of seeing the economy, originally expounded by economists from Austria. Following custom, we refer to the theory as Austrian, not Hayekian.)

Frederick A. Hayek

An Austrian Version of the Business Cycle

A simplified Austrian version of the business cycle is a story of how government intervention affects interest rates, which distorts savings and investment decisions, i.e., the property cycle. Entrepreneurial errors in the property cycle ultimately cause a failure in the economy, with lost production and unemployment.

A key insight of the Austrian story is a recognition that it takes time to develop new business investments. Some businesses, such as a coffee shop, can become productive in a short time, weeks or months. Other businesses, such as a nuclear power plant, may take years to build out the specialized capital required. In order to achieve the most efficient production processes, it may take a long time to build specialized equipment. The longer it takes to build specialized capital, the more potential there is for error. Perhaps the entrepreneur misjudges the market demand. Perhaps technological advances will obviate the need for the product. There are many things that can change profitability, when the development period stretches over years and even decades.

Because of the extra riskiness of long development times, businesses demand a higher profit on long term investment, compared to that on projects that are producing profits in just a short period. Because these long-term projects are expected to be more efficient, they should be able to earn higher profits. Interest rates are therefore normally higher for long term borrowing than for short term borrowing.

In the Austrian theory of business cycles, interest rates play a major role in allocating savings to various investment projects. High interest rates are an indication of scarce savings. Entrepreneurs have to compete harder for investment funds, and households require a greater incentive to save. It will take a good profit opportunity, with a high rate of return, to convince households to divert money into savings. These are distinctive elements of Austrian theory: the development time structure of capital, "roundabout" production methods and so on, that are important contributions to economic theory.

Suppose an entrepreneur is inspired by an innovative idea. She needs to borrow funds for investment in this new project. To attract funds from other possible investments into her own project, she must offer a higher interest rate. Because of her confidence in the profitability of the idea, she is willing to offer a higher interest rate. Households, responding to a higher interest rate, increase savings to fund her plans.

Increased savings means there is an equivalent reduction of money spent on consumption. Firms respond to lower consumption by reducing production of consumer goods and services, thereby reducing employment of production workers. The story does not end with increased unemployment and recession, however. The savings taken out of the production cycle are put into the property cycle. Entrepreneurs use the funds to purchase capital goods, which increases employment in the production of capital goods, and they hire construction workers to build the new projects. Theoretically, all resources continue to be employed. In fact, labor is specialized, and laid off production workers are not the same people as newly hired construction workers. But with an allowance of time for adjustment, all resources are employed.

New business projects introduce innovations that increase productivity and the standard of living. Greater productivity provides the rate of return needed to pay interest on savings, which also provides income to buy the increased production. There is a dynamic equilibrium, with a rising standard of living.

Suppose an entrepreneur makes a mistake; the project is a failure. Suppose there is no increased productivity, no return on investment. If the loss is an insignificant portion of the economy, then the loss is absorbed as if nothing happened. Yes, resources are wasted, but there is no lingering effect. If the loss is significant, where many entrepreneurs make the same mistake (such as the housing boom and bust 1996-2008—see below), then a longer time is required to absorb the losses, which we call a recession. Households need time to restore lost savings, which tends to reduce consumption, production, and employment. Eventually, the economy heals itself. Interest rates decrease, which spurs new business investment and capital goods purchases to rise. Less consumer spending causes prices to fall, which ultimately increases demand for consumer goods too, and production increases in the production cycle. With time, the economy is restored to health.

A problem arises when entrepreneurs are fooled into making mistakes because of actions by the government. For example, suppose the government intervenes in the economy to keep interest rates unnaturally low. In response to lower interest rates, entrepreneurs increase demand for investment resources. Unnaturally low interest rates, depressed by government actions to increase money and credit, make long term projects relatively more attractive than short term projects. According to Austrian theory, low interest rates which result from government intervention, not from consumer behavior or entrepreneurial behavior, will induce excess investment in longer term projects. Ultimately, in the Austrian theory, artificially induced long-term projects are more likely to fail than projects induced by market-tested demand.

In the short run, government supplied easy money and credit will create a boom in the economy. Entrepreneurs purchase capital goods and hire construction workers to build projects. Households increase consumption. Firms hire more workers to meet the demand for more consumer and capital goods. Workers are in short supply, so wages rise, spurring incomes and demand even higher. For a while it appears that government intervention has "worked." But excessive investment ultimately results in the production of too many goods. To sell the glut of goods, prices fall below the cost of production, profits turn to losses, household savings are wiped out, demand for consumption goods declines, production and employment are cut, which further reduces household income. The business cycle is at the bottom point. Eventually the excess supply is extinguished, prices stop falling, profits return, and the economy begins to heal itself. The Austrian business cycle is complete.

An example of an Austrian style business cycle is the housing boom that ended with the collapse of house prices, and nearly the collapse of the financial system in October 2008. Government intervention by the Clinton Administration and then the Bush Administration greatly expanded easy credit to lower middle class homebuyers, on extremely loose terms. The result was a decade of over-building in housing. Eventually the supply of new homes far exceeded the number of truly qualified buyers, and the housing boom was over in 2007. House prices fell, losses accumulated, and many banks failed.

Subprime Mortgage Originations

In 2006, $600 billion of subprime loans were originated, most of which were securitized. That year, subprime lending accounted for 23.5% of all mortgage originations.

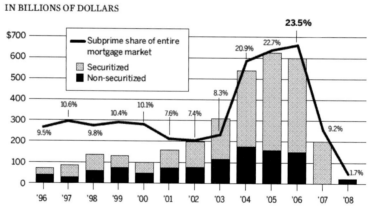

NOTE: Percent securitized is defined as subprime securities issued divided by originations in a given year. In 2007, securities issued exceeded originations.

SOURCE: Inside Mortgage Finance

The Production, Property & Power model is largely consistent with Austrian theory. Austrian theory, like the PP&P model, emphasizes the role and centrality of inter-temporal economic decision-making. The PP&P model does not try to segment time into longer and shorter development time, which is a feature of the Austrian theory. The PP&P model, unlike Austrian theory, includes psychological motives for decision-makers. The PP&P model includes the government as an integral part of the economic model, whereas Austrian theory considers government an external intervention. Overall though, the Austrian theory and the PP&P model have much in common.

The Keynesian Version of the Business Cycle

Keynes emphasized that there are psychological influences in the economy. He famously characterized the business confidence of bankers and entrepreneurs as "animal spirits." He observed that when entrepreneurs have little confidence in the economy, they do not invest in new business projects, despite low interest rates. Whereas Austrian theory predicts entrepreneurs will take advantage of low interest rates, Keynes emphasized that first they needed to restore "animal spirits." Overcoming this psychological barrier is the objective of Keynesian economics.

John Maynard Keynes

Keynes introduced a way of thinking about the economy in the aggregate—what today we call macroeconomics. At the aggregate level there is only one economic decision-maker, the government controller. Keynesian economics is about relationships that are observed between aggregate variables (e.g., unemployment rates, GDP, etc.). These relationships are believed to be valid and reliable for policy decisions. The government controller uses knowledge of these relationships to "manage" the economy.

For example, one of the (sometimes) observed relationships is a short-term inverse relationship between inflation and unemployment, known as the Phillips Curve. When inflation increases, unemployment is expected to decrease in the near term and vice versa. Another important observation is what Keynes called the marginal propensity to consume. This is the portion of additional income that is spent, not saved. In the aggregate, Keynesian theory believes this to be a stable portion. There are many other, more intricate relationships and interconnections, in modern Keynesian economics. Keynesian economics is a theory of stimulus-response, with no inter-temporal importance other than lag effects before the expected response to the stimulus occurs.

At the heart of basic Keynesian economics are the importance of consumption and the danger of over-saving. Since households consume a fixed portion of additional income (the marginal propensity to consume), then an increase in household income will give rise to a predictable increase in consumption. Better than that, the income devoted to increased consumption will cycle through the economy, creating more income and consumption each time it cycles through. This concept is called the consumption multiplier, where an increase in government spending increases total income by more than dollar for dollar. There is no corresponding savings multiplier, since according to the Keynesian version, the portion of income allocated to savings is idle, piling up uselessly in savings accounts or worse, in home mattresses. Since entrepreneurs are paralyzed by low confidence, there is no demand for investment resources; savings sit idle. Savings do not cycle through the economy, instead savings drain money out of the production cycle. Keynes argued that there was too much thrift in the economy, to the point of harming the economy; the so-called paradox of thrift.

Keynes proposed that the government controller intervene to put idle savings to work in the economy. The government could issue debt to soak up the idle savings and use the borrowed funds in some way to get them back to work. Keynes himself favored public investment in infrastructure, but he was not adamant on this point. He believed so strongly in the harm of idle savings that he overstated the need for government deficit spending, even to the point of frivolous government spending. Politicians since Keynes have had many ideas of how to spend borrowed idle savings, including many frivolous ones. According to Keynes, government spending didn't have to be productive, it just had to increase spending, what he called aggregate demand. Once injected into the economy, the consumption multiplier would increase the impact of government spending, even if frivolous, and the economy would be stimulated back to life. Business confidence would return to entrepreneurs, demand for investment resources would return, savings would no longer be idle, and equilibrium would be restored.

Keynesian ideas have been dominant among economists since 1936. The basic ideas are still orthodox policy for policymakers in both major parties. Unfortunately, Keynes did not account for a lack of fiscal discipline on the part of politicians. Economies that follow Keynesian policies are therefore covered in a blanket of government debt.

Supply-Side Economics

During the 1970s, Keynesian economic theory was challenged by inflation, and another thread of economics developed known as supply-side economics.

Arthur Laffer

Arthur Laffer (of the Laffer Curve), an economic advisor to President Reagan, brought supply-side economics into public policy. A key criticism of Keynesian economics made by supply-side economics is that demand management (i.e., typical Keynesian policies) ignores the important role of incentives on the production side of the economy.

Supply-siders emphasized policy actions that increase incentives to increase savings and business investment, not simply to increase consumption. An increase in business investment would put idle savings to work, just like deficit spending, but with more market-guided projects and less opportunity for frivolous government spending. Supply-side economics lies between Keynesian and Austrian economics. It still deals mostly with aggregate variables, but supply-siders are more likely to consider the response of entrepreneurs and households when crafting policy actions.

The PP&P model differs from Keynesian macroeconomics. Keynesian theory focuses on the decisions of the government controller. In Keynesian macroeconomics, there are mechanistic relationships, with lags perhaps, but no market forces and the future is mostly ignored. Keynesians are almost exclusively present oriented. As Keynes famously said, "In the long run we are all dead." In contrast, the PP&P model is based on market forces and psychological forces that act inter-temporally on households and entrepreneurs. The future is a significant factor in the decisions made by households and entrepreneurs in the present.

An episode from the George W. Bush administration illustrates a difference between a Keynesian perspective and the PP&P model. On two occasions, the Bush administration chose to inject a Keynesian dose of "borrow and spend" stimulus into the economy by paying "tax rebate" checks to taxpayers. While this was essentially Keynesian policy to increase aggregate demand, the tax rebate mechanism gave the stimulus a supply-side flavor. Some Keynesian economists criticized the decision to use tax rebates instead of government directed spending. If the government had spent the money itself, then 100% of the spending would have been injected into the production cycle. But since actual spending was left up to the individual, a portion would be "wasted" in increased savings (mostly to pay off credit card debts), according to the critics.

From the perspective of the PP&P model, the portion of the Bush tax rebate that was used to pay down credit card debt is consistent with the household motivation to reduce fear and anxiety. The tax rebate used to pay down debt reduces anxiety, and shortens the time for household choices to return to "normal" after a recession-induced spike in fear. Debt repayment is not "wasted," in the perspective of the PP&P model. It is calming, it speeds up the healing time. More government spending might actually raise anxiety and lengthen the recession, especially if the government is seen to be spending foolishly.

Which perspective is the right one? Opinions will differ, but the debate sharpens insights. In Appendix B, we use the PP&P model to give us insight into how the policy might work in the case of solving the looming problem of Social Security insolvency.

Appendix B

Using the PP&P Model to Analyze Public Policy

SOCIAL SECURITY

Background

Social Security was enacted in 1935 as a funded public pension plan. A special tax on wages was intended to create a retirement reserve fund that would be sufficient to provide old-age pensions. Each generation of workers would fund their own retirement security. That plan was quickly amended, in 1939, to do away with advance funding, and change Social Security to a pay-as-you-go system, also known as paygo. Under paygo, taxes are used immediately to provide benefits to current retirees. (A relatively small Trust Fund was built up to smooth out size differences between generations.)

In the past thirty years however, there has been unexpected improvement in survival rates at ages above 60 and a decrease in the number of children per family. As a result of these demographic factors, the Social Security tax rate is out of date. The system does not collect enough in taxes to pay the benefits it has promised. According to the Social Security Trustees Report of 2019, the Trust Fund will be exhausted by 2035. Once the Trust Fund is exhausted, Social Security taxes will only pay for about 75% of promised benefits. (The impact on government spending of inadequate Social Security taxes will be felt well before 2035. By 2020, the cost of Social Security benefits will exceed

total income. The shortfall will have to be made up by depleting the Trust Fund, causing the federal government to pay for its own spending by raising taxes, cutting government spending elsewhere, or increasing the deficit.)

Social Security pensions are intended to replace about 35-40% of the average worker's pre-retirement income. The pension formula replaces up to 90% of wages for low income workers (below 20% of the national average wage), 35% of wages for middle income workers, and less for high wage workers (15% of wages above 125% of the national average and 0% for wages above $136,000). Social Security was intended to be a portion of a worker's total retirement income, together with personal savings, and company provided pensions.

Congress has cut Social Security benefits several times, either by raising the retirement age, or by raising taxes on the pension benefit. From the unpopular menu choices of raising taxes, cutting benefits, or a combination of both, Congress will have to construct a solution to the inevitable impasse of not enough money to pay for promised pensions.

Social Security also includes disability and survivor benefits. We will only consider here the old age pension portion of Social Security. We will analyze how the Production, Property & Power model of the economy can help us understand the effect of Social Security policy on the economy.

Social Security and Households

Households have no choice but to pay Social Security taxes. Jack, the household decision-maker, is confident that Social Security will provide old-age income, so he won't need to save up as much in his nest egg as he would have accumulated without Social Security. The money that he would have put toward his nest egg is used instead to pay the Social Security tax. Jack does not need to reduce consumption to pay the Social Security tax; he reduces savings instead. In the end, the household saves less, consumes about the same, pays Social Security tax, and has about the same level of anxiety about retirement and satisfaction from consumption as before. The main outcome of paygo Social

Security for Jack has been to replace the ownership of accumulated property in a household nest egg with a government promise backed by current taxes.

Total savings in the economy are reduced, since a goodly portion of resources that would have gone to savings has gone instead to pay taxes. Those taxes provide benefits for current retirees, who tend to spend rather than save the income. Overall savings are therefore significantly reduced. (Social Security negatively affects income inequality, family cohesion, fertility rates, and other important effects. These are beyond the scope of this analysis.)

Social Security and Entrepreneurs

Paygo Social Security reduces the amount of savings available for banks to lend to entrepreneurs like Tom. Banks pay higher rates of interest to attract savings. Tom can move ahead with his innovation if he is confident it will earn a high enough return to make a profit despite the higher interest rates. Some projects are cancelled due to lack of funds. Over the years, the accumulated effect of low savings will be less growth, less development of innovation, and less accumulated capital. Arguably, paygo Social Security might result in a lower standard of living than what would have been with a higher savings rate.

We cannot know the projects that were not built and the innovations that were not pursued due to the scarcity of savings. Because we cannot know what might have been, does not mean we should ignore this hidden cost of paygo Social Security.

Social Security and Politicians

Social Security has been one of the most popular government programs of all time. Perhaps that is because citizens have been unable to properly assess its true value and true cost, given that benefits are not supported by current tax rates. But perhaps Social Security provides so much utility value by reducing anxiety over old age poverty that it deserves its high standing among the public, even with its low money's worth return on taxes.

For more than eighty years, households cut back on savings to pay Social Security taxes, leaving households dependent on government for security. (A recent report from Pew Charitable Trusts found that 1 in 3 families has *no* savings.) Under a paygo design, there is no investment return to help pay the cost of pension benefits. The entire cost of benefits are paid by current workers.

Assuming politicians fix Social Security in a way that preserves its current structure (i.e., tax increases and benefit cuts to make the system sound, but no fundamental redesign), then Social Security will require a tax of about 15%

of wages. That tax revenue becomes "out of reach" of politicians for any other plans they might have.

The so-called entitlement programs of Disability Insurance, Medicare, and Obamacare are also competing with other government priorities for a share of the total tax extracted from households. As all the entitlements press on tax revenues, politicians face tough choices. The government can attempt to squeeze out more revenue by continuing to raise tax rates, at a high cost to individual liberty and at a declining level of effectiveness as per the Laffer Curve. Without more tax revenues to pay for the rising cost of entitlements, there will be less revenue left for defense, for administration of justice, or other government services. The PP&P model shows that politicians will increasingly feel the stress of Laffer-constrained revenues as the promises of entitlements come due and must be addressed.

Social Security has no upside for politicians, there is only downside. Households have adjusted their savings plan to the promised benefits, taxes have been paid for 80+ years, and there is only political danger if politicians reduce benefits or increase taxes. That share of taxing capacity under the Laffer Curve is "lost" to politicians. It will be dangerous for any politician to reclaim those revenues for any other purpose.

Summary of the Effect of Social Security

Social Security has promised highly valued old-age security benefits to households. But it has unintended side effects. Social Security has redirected economy-wide resources away from savings and investment and into consumption. While difficult to assess the damage, it is possible, even likely, that due to lower savings and investment, there is more wealth inequality, less capital accumulation, less innovation, and a lower standard of living today than might have been the case without paygo Social Security. People are living longer and having fewer children than expected. Consequently, the tax rate for paygo Social Security is inadequate to provide the promised benefits. Politicians face hard choices and the constraints of the Laffer Curve as they debate how to solve the problem of paygo Social Security.

The Production, Property & Power model is useful to gain deeper insight into how public policy might affect the economy. Too often, public policy is discussed with attention only on the direct impact of the policy. The advantage of understanding the economy with a mental framework such as the PP&P model is that public policy can be discussed in a broader context of how it will affect all the sectors of the economy as people adjust their behavior over time to the new policy. The model is too simple to form strong beliefs about policy, but it is a rich enough model to raise important issues for further analysis.

NOTES

PRODUCTION, PROPERTY & POWER MODEL